SASHA SWEDER

This Doesn't Make Me An Expert

and other lies I have told myself while building a successful direct sales business.

Third edition

ISBN: 979-8-9902618-1-5

Editing by David Sweder
Editing by Ronna Lebo
Editing by Rob Pastorio

This book was professionally typeset on Reedsy.
Find out more at reedsy.com

Dedicated to my hubby & kids.
You can do scary things; I'll always be cheering for you.

Contents

1

Take The Chance

No one tells you how people around you will react to your decision to start a business with a direct sales company. I often, jokingly, compare it to the first few moments after telling people close to you that you are marrying a guy no one likes or having a baby when everyone thinks it is too soon. It all starts with a peaceful room announcement where everyone is watching or maybe a social media status that feels anxiety-filled. Next comes the reaction of hesitant smiles and "congratulations" that friends share because they have listened to 30 seconds of what you said but are confident that whatever you say is a HAPPY statement. Everyone lets out a resounding "Congrats!" and then comes the "well-intended" Q&A session, where people try to pinpoint the flaws in your plan in a public forum until you second guess if you should be as excited as you are.

"So, have you picked a date for the wedding?" is an excellent way of saying, *"Pick the month I did, or you are wrong because December is reserved for marriages that last. I am not biased; I happened to be married in December."* Or the, "So excited you are having a baby! Are you going to breastfeed?" which is equivalent to, *"Boob is best, bottles are for quitters, and I know this because I have a dog that I read graphic novels to and I watched a TikTok."* In this case, the question will be, "So excited you are starting a business, but isn't that one of those pyramid schemes?" The question cuts like a knife, right to the point, and tends to come from a family member or friend packed with well-intended concern.

Many businesses die before they even start because of the scary situation where you are face to face with people doubting your decisions. This is the moment when you have to make a choice. Do you let anxiety kick in and question everything you have done to this point, or do you get down to business and make good on your highly anticipated public announcement? It is time to get started! I understand that starting a business can be a daunting task, and planning for it can be overwhelming. That's why I want to remind you that there may be moments when you feel unsure or stuck, especially when using your computer or platform. But please don't worry; I'm here to help you every step of the way. Together, we can overcome challenges and make your business dreams a reality. You may be met with the crippling fears that cause some of the strongest people I know to crumble or quit. Fears of judgment from family and friends, fear from society telling you that you made a poor choice, worries about finances, or fears of inadequacy when you keep hearing NO from your most vital support system. The thing to keep in mind is this is not abnormal for any business opportunity. Whether opening a pizza place, toy store, or direct sales business, many go through this exact moment.

Unfortunately, so many are misinformed or have had bad experiences with direct sales that they can't give you five minutes to sit and be excited, scared, or whatever you feel. These questions come from decades of stories of friends and family members falling for "get rich quick" schemes and seeing newscasts or documentaries about the scary aftereffects of companies that broke the law, were dishonest, made crappy products, and sold consultants a ton of lies. Direct selling is woven into our society when we see requests for direct sales company products like SkinSoSoft for military members to protect from bugs in the field, Disney partnering with Scentsy Wax to bring magic home, Tupperware for lunches on the shelves at Target, or Pampered Chef kitchen tools on TV cooking segments regularly. This makes me wonder whether the products entice people to join a company. The answer is no; it's not the products but how people treat each other more often. You may find yourself surrounded by snakes or flowers, but you will need a guide to show you how not to be taken for a fool. Remember, direct sales is like any other flawed industry.

I have been with three companies since I initially wrote this book. The first company I had to leave after a scandalous merger. The second closed the doors on us without warning after a successful holiday season, and the third company has been great. In all my experience, I have seen people take advantage of policies, companies fail to pay out checks, friendships break over money, and false promises for incentive trips. It can be rough and has drawbacks; however, this can be a rewarding and lucrative industry. Without the many opportunities presented to me throughout my career in direct sales, I would never have gone parasailing, made lifelong friendships I can count on, presented in front of over 1,000 people on stage, and led a team to sell over 18 million dollars in soap during a pandemic while raising my two kids. The blessings were worth it: It is what you make of it.

A Short History of Direct Sales

Direct sales companies in the United States have deep historical roots, dating back to the late 19th century. The concept gained traction with the establishment of the Fuller Brush Company in 1906 by Alfred C. Fuller, partially now known as the Sara Lee Corporation. Using a door-to-door sales approach, Fuller Brush became a pioneer in the industry, selling high-quality brushes directly to consumers. This marked the beginning of a new era where companies recognized the potential of reaching customers directly in their homes. In the early to mid-20th century, direct sales saw the emergence of iconic companies that are still household names today.

Avon, founded in 1886, became a trailblazer by empowering women to become sales representatives, offering them a chance at financial independence. The company underwent a significant shift in 1939, changing its name to Avon Products, Inc. Inspired by the success of women in direct selling, Avon became a household name in enabling women to become entrepreneurs and sales representatives.

Mary Kay, established in 1963, followed a similar path, focusing on beauty products and creating a unique incentive system, including the famous Pink Cadillac reward. Mary Kay Ash founded Mary Kay Cosmetics in 1963 after experiencing gender discrimination in the workplace. Her vision was to create a company allowing women to achieve personal and financial success. One of Mary Kay's most iconic traditions is the Pink Cadillac incentive. Top-performing sales consultants have been rewarded with pink Cadillacs, symbolizing success and dedication.

Tupperware revolutionized direct sales in the 1950s by introducing the concept of home parties, transforming how kitchen products were marketed and sold. Tupperware, founded by Earl Tupper, gained prominence in the post-World War II era with the invention of airtight plastic containers. However, the products faced challenges in traditional retail settings due to their unique nature. Tupperware's breakthrough came in the 1950s when Brownie Wise, a saleswoman, introduced the concept of home parties. This innovative approach allowed Tupperware to be demonstrated and sold directly to consumers in a social setting.

A notable aspect of the direct sales history in the U.S. is its impact on women's entrepreneurship. Avon and Mary Kay, in particular, played significant roles in providing women with opportunities to build their businesses and achieve financial success. These companies offered quality products and fostered a sense of community and empowerment among their sales representatives. As technology advanced, the direct sales model adapted to changing consumer behaviors. In the 21st century, they witnessed the integration of online platforms and social media into the landscape of direct sales. Companies like Amway, Herbalife, and Young Living embraced digital tools to complement traditional methods, enabling representatives to connect with a broader audience and conduct business virtually.

Amway, short for "American Way," was founded by Jay Van Andel and Richard DeVos in 1959. It has grown into one of the largest direct-selling companies globally, offering various products, including health and wellness items, home care, and beauty products. Founded by Mark Hughes in 1980, Herbalife specializes in nutrition, weight management, and personal care products. The company has gained prominence for its network marketing approach involving independent Consultants. Young Living, established by Gary Young in 1993, is renowned for its essential oils and wellness products. The company emphasizes the benefits of natural and pure essential oils and has a direct sales model with a network of independent Consultants. These companies, Avon, Mary Kay, and Tupperware, have played significant roles in shaping the direct sales landscape. Each has its unique product offerings and business strategies, contributing to the diversity of the direct selling industry.

Direct sales continue to thrive in the United States, with various companies representing various industries. The enduring legacy of pioneers like Amway, Avon, Fuller Brush, Herbalife, Mary Kay, Tupperware, and Young Living is evident in the ongoing success of direct selling as a business model. Despite the evolution of marketing strategies, direct sales remains a dynamic way for companies to connect with consumers personally, providing products and opportunities directly to their doorstep.

Let's Untangle Confusing Terms

Before we delve further, let's untangle some commonly mixed-up terms. Have you ever felt that uneasy twinge when you hear *Madoff Investment Securities* or *Metabolife*? Now, try *Pampered Chef* on for size. I bet you're feeling more cozy and confident towards *Pampered Chef*, imagining those trusty kitchen gadgets. Unlike the former two, your gut instinct is that Pampered Chef won't land you in hot water; it's more likely to help you whip up a comforting bowl of soup.

So, what's the difference in dealing with these companies? Let's start with the scariest of the bunch: the pyramid scheme that made Madoff Financial Securities and Metabolife infamous. According to Britannica.com and the Federal Trade Commission(FTC), a pyramid scheme is like a financial game of Jenga, promising quick cash but inevitably causing the tower to topple, leaving players empty-handed. It's the "too good to be true" trap many fall for and lose life investments. It's all smoke and mirrors, promising riches but delivering disappointment and jail time. The issue with pyramid schemes is they are not always shaped like a pyramid. One version I saw was the social media post where everyone in your following sends you a dollar, but then you send them a dollar and get nothing in return. That's the essence of a traditional pyramid scheme: you put money in and get nothing you were promised in return.

In contrast, there's affiliate marketing, direct sales, network marketing, and multi-level marketing (MLM). The FTC defines direct selling as the art of peddling wares person-to-person, whether from the comfort of your home or through social media. Direct Sales is selling products manufactured by a wholesaler or retailer and convincing your network to buy that fancy blender you swear by or sharing a link for an item you love after signing up directly with a retailer. When you do that, you get a percentage paid to you as commissions from the company, potentially have 1099 around tax time as an independent contractor if you earned more than $600 in commissions, and owe taxes at the end of the year based on your sales and the sales of your teammates.

Do you get paid for a starter kit from a credible Direct Sales company? No. You only get paid bonuses when they sell to their customers. Later, we will talk about what happens if your leader teaches you to do something like purchasing large amounts of stock, making promises to you of extravagant income, or claiming their products cure illnesses, which can then move legitimate businesses down illegal avenues.

Direct Selling Companies can take on many forms, like pyramid schemes, making it very hard for a consumer or salesperson to understand everything they are signing up for in advance adequately. Still, the trick is knowing how to maneuver strategically to protect you and your team from people without your best interests. For this book, we'll discuss tangible products—things you can hold, smell, and, most importantly, sell without fear of ending up on the evening news. Let's face it: nobody wants their mom calling to bail them out of jail.

Do You Have a Startup Business?
One of the most common objections people have told me while in this business in the last 11 years is, "You will never be a real business." Many

will question the validity of your business before you even open. To help you overcome this, let's first really define what a business is. 'Business' generally includes any activity to produce income from selling goods or performing services. In the eyes of the government and my friend, the IRS, as soon as you start earning money in your favorite side hustle, you're a business and considered a "sole proprietor." Individuals who provide a service and collect money from it are sole proprietors. Many businesses start this way, and many don't need to be anything else. Some of the leaders I have worked with eventually morphed into LLCs, but that is a story for another chapter. As stated, the companies you are deciding to join have proven track records of making an impact with consultants, but does that translate to you 'owning' anything you build? The answer will surprise you if you think it does not!

A more specific version of this objection is, "You will never be a real business unless you have a storefront." That statement shows you already that the person you are talking to has a set picture in their head of what a business looks like from the outside. It immediately ignores all of the progress that craft, digital products, or service-based companies have had online in the last ten years, but let's focus on "direct sales vs a storefront."

Over the last 5-10 years, the rise of online shopping has been nothing short of revolutionary, reshaping the retail landscape globally. The accessibility of smartphones, improved internet connectivity, and a shift in consumer preferences have fueled the massive growth of e-commerce. Major players like Amazon, Alibaba, and other online marketplaces have become synonymous with the convenience and accessibility that online shopping offers. The COVID-19 pandemic further accelerated this trend as lockdowns and safety concerns prompted a surge in digital transactions. Consumers now enjoy many products at their fingertips, often with expedited delivery options. The rise of mobile applications, streamlined payment processes, and personalized shopping experiences have made online shopping more efficient and created a seismic shift in how businesses operate and consumers make purchasing decisions. As technology continues to advance, the trajectory of online shopping is likely to persist, with an ongoing impact on traditional brick-and-mortar retail models.

The rapid rise of online shopping over the past decade has also significantly influenced the landscape of direct sales, ushering in a new era of convenience and accessibility. Direct sales companies have embraced the digital realm, providing their representatives with online platforms for seamless transactions. The convenience of ordering products online has expanded the reach of direct sales companies and empowered their sales force to connect with customers. Social media, e-commerce websites, and personalized online portals have become integral tools for direct sales representatives, offering a dynamic and interactive space to showcase products, engage with customers, and facilitate transactions. This digital evolution in direct sales has not only streamlined the buying process for consumers but has also enhanced the efficiency and effectiveness of the direct sales model, allowing representatives to leverage the power of online ordering and digital marketing to grow their businesses. As the trend of online shopping continues to shape consumer behavior, integrating e-commerce into direct sales is poised to play an increasingly pivotal role in the industry's ongoing success.

Can you even make money?

Another significant objection that has come up fast has been, "You will never make any money off that." The hard part of this allegation is that it comes with accountability and commitment to build or treat the opportunity as a hobby, like getting a gym membership doesn't immediately promise you the perfect body. You buy the kit but must bring the business to life.

Direct sales typically have low startup costs compared to traditional businesses. With minimal investment in inventory or equipment, individuals can start their direct sales venture without significant upfront expenses. This makes it accessible for individuals looking to start a business with limited capital. Not everyone has the economic resources to pour soap, purchase a monogramming machine to label luggage or create a line of cookware. A brand-new brick-and-mortar business requires legal documentation to register & license your business, advertising, bookkeeping, branding, furnishing, insurance, inventory, a location you own or rent, personnel training, printing, staffing, utilities, and website services.

On the other hand, direct sales companies alleviate the costs of the requirements to start a business in sales. The starter kit costs are invested into the necessary training to work a business successfully, pay your commissions on sales, manage product inventory shipping, and manage all the other costly overhead associated with running a storefront. Even fewer have the financial resources to set up a storefront in an economy where it is estimated that the majority of people purchase online vs in their neighborhood stores. The affordable convenience of direct sales starter kits compared to opening a brick-and-mortar store gives people more access to income outside of starting from scratch. No one thinks that a restaurant buying tomato sauce from a supplies vendor is not legit as a restaurant. All you are doing is buying a kit to sell a product line. It is the 'tomato sauce' you are offering to your customers.

But a direct sales business is like any other business; you need to know when you break even and when you need to invest intelligently. I will be very direct about this: Direct Sales hobbyists rarely calculate Return on Investment (ROI) or budget like a business; a clear example is advertising outside their warm markets. One of the first calculations I made when I got my kit for $99 was how long it took me to earn that $99 back. Like any other business, it's essential to calculate ROI in direct sales. This involves tracking expenses for product purchases, marketing materials, travel to training events, and other business-related costs. By comparing these expenses to the income generated from sales, representatives can assess the profitability of their business and make informed decisions to optimize their ROI. Proper budgeting and financial management are critical for success in direct sales. This includes setting aside funds for product purchases, marketing initiatives, training, and other business expenses.

As my business and team grew, I learned it was much closer to a "real" business opportunity than I had ever been told, but I had to be careful and strategic. Spending everything I made on more products or supplies was very tempting, but I had to resist that to grow. I had to apply what I will teach you in this book to protect and educate myself, my family, and my team. I HATE Excel spreadsheets and have had to learn so much more than I ever wanted to. I have made expensive mistakes and had to find a way to rally our team with $5 in my bank account to finish out the month strong despite those mistakes. I learned how to read reports for patterns, take notes in meetings to reference later, and break down complex business operations lessons into bite-size pieces for those who needed the knowledge.

Lucrative businesses recognize they need to expand past their inner circles to succeed. Some who start a direct sales business assume that friends and family are their core customers and do not realize the world must be more significant to progress. They spam the ten people they know well who have shown interest for years and exhaust them without reaching out of their circle. This can mimic the results of a person opening a pizza place from your kitchen and expecting only your family to buy pizza for all three meals for decades. Unrealistic and dangerous financial decisions will ensue either way! *Also, gastrointestinal because that is a lot of pizza. Treat both opportunities equally when* comparing the two options because both can turn disastrous. No matter what business you open, if your family and close friends are the only ones buying from you, it is time to pound some pavement to get the word out.

Direct sales companies offer flexibility in terms of working hours and efforts invested. Representatives can choose how much time and energy they want to dedicate to their business, allowing for work-life balance and pursuing other interests or responsibilities. In my experience, this promise of flexibility is a half-truth. Many misunderstood that *flexibility* as a promise of income with inconsistent effort and minimal time dedicated to working. This type of business doesn't run itself and can stop short if you do not invest time in fostering relationships. You have to plant seeds like any other business. Some see the time they sit and watch for posts in chats & team pages as the time they used to work their business that day, but it is not. You will not get a return if you are not spending the time you dedicate to growing a customer list, making connections, or selling. You will only get rewarded for the time you spend doing business-focused activities.

Depending on the company you join and the team you build, you need to decide what you want in return and how much time you are willing to invest to get that return. The more effort and time put into sales activities, the higher the potential income. If you treat this like a real business, you can make real money. If you treat this like a hobby or the gym membership you forgot you had, it will not. But that's your choice!

Rejection happens.

The last main objective I want to cover before moving forward is from people who are considering joining a direct sales company but hate rejection. I have learned that rejection is more about them than me, and I have become desensitized. Through all the No's in my life, the only time they stopped me from achieving was when I let them block me from seeing a path forward, and that happened way more often than I would like to admit.

Others will project their fears onto you. People kept telling me it wouldn't work out, and at first, I believed them because it was a habit to believe others before listening to my intuition. Honestly, I am not even confident I knew what "working out" looked like without seeing the success stories of others who traveled before me. I had to learn that roadblocks required more creativity and innovation. It is my job to figure out how to get it done anyway, especially if I believe that what I am fighting for is important and connects with my overall vision for how I want my life.

After a short time, people could say whatever they wanted; we were a business. It was irrelevant because I had numbers to prove (not once, not twice, but three times) that opinions about my type of business were inaccurate if done well. It became a battle of the views versus facts, and the facts won. The effort to always fight back against it or become defensive wasted my energy. I stopped myself short of my goals on so many occasions because I believed that other people had the right to tell me where to go, how to sit, what I could do, and when I could do it. I could have often corrected people who thought I was lazy, stubborn, or selfish, but I also learned that was pointless.

Get focused.

Direct sales can change your life if you manage it like a real business, or it can cost you a ton, beat you down, and put you in debt that only emotional choices can create. This is a mental game. There are trap doors, slides backward, and power-ups like any other game, but making the wrong move in this one can cost you a lot in real life. If you believe you can not do this ethically, refuse to learn how to, and then give up, then yes, you will fail before you even hit join on the website.

In this industry, you can control your destiny. People will try to convince you that you do not, but you do. You may have an upline leader that helps you, but you are your driver. What you do when you get off that training meeting is the real meat and potatoes of this opportunity. It is not what you do when the corporate executives are standing next to you; it is what you do when you get home from that event. I have seen people who never attended events hit the top ranks of a pay plan by educating themselves in business practices and implementing them. I have stood up tall in rooms that didn't see me as deserving to be in them and learned you must take yourself seriously way before those around you consider you worthy of what you earn or receive. You must invest in yourself, be proud and excited about yourself, and motivate yourself. You must push yourself when it isn't easy because it won't always be paychecks and magic. You must recognize how far you have come because others will never see your full potential. You must also stay humble to stay productive because a tax spreadsheet can smell fear, and customers do not care about your title if you give lousy customer service. You can have your entire company implode and start over as often as needed. You can fall and get back up. You can even leave with a massive amount of knowledge, business experience, and an entire base of people cheering you on, ready to create a traditional retail business and succeed off the info you learned while working in this business. The possibilities are endless and worth the calculated risk.

Direct selling can be one of the scariest, most beautiful, and most challenging endeavors you will ever embark upon. The lessons in this book were learned from hard-fought years of experience and helped shape me into the business person I am now. I can't wait to help you grow. Let's go!

2

People are Your Business

I begged people for years to tell me what my job description was. It was overwhelming to notice that I wore the hat for almost every single aspect of the business, including finance & tax accountant, sales representative, brand marketing, human resources, customer service, and product advertising, to name a few. Then it hit me: It is your job to help people. It is your job to introduce the brand, the products, and the experience. However, you must have people to help; that is where networking comes into play. Networking with people is the foundation of the business and your success. My job begins and ends with how well I can help people, whether they are buying my products or selling them.

When you accept that people are the business, you recognize that communication is essential for that business to be profitable. How you connect, educate, or collaborate will determine whether or not you are successful. Communication dictates how you will reach out to those who want information, product samples or want to learn.

Imagine, if you will, your entire direct sales career is a string of parties from launch to retirement. The list of people you meet and continue to network with will gradually grow, and they will be the ones you invite to every 'party' you plan. Over time, you will amass a collection of people to include in every move, from celebrating milestones to sharing product updates. Throughout your sales career, this list should grow as you do and resemble the demographic of people who have been with you on the journey, know your brand, trust you to advocate for them, and "love your vibe," as the kids say.

Your Quick Crash Course in the 3 Ps of Service

Marcus Lemonis, a successful business owner and investor with a net worth exceeding 1 billion dollars, often discusses a crucial management principle for your business: The 3 Ps. The PPP framework offers a comprehensive approach to improving your organization by focusing on three key areas: people, process, and product. By taking a holistic view of these areas, you can identify opportunities for improvement and develop strategies to enhance performance.

Understanding the three Ps is also essential for success in sales. First and foremost, having in-depth knowledge of your product enables you to effectively communicate its features, benefits, and value proposition to potential customers. This understanding helps build confidence and credibility, which is vital for establishing trust and driving sales. Second, mastering the sales process—from prospecting to closing—is crucial. A structured approach ensures smooth interactions, the ability to address objections, and guiding prospects through the buying journey. Lastly, recognizing the importance of people involves understanding your customers' needs, motivations, and behaviors. Building strong relationships based on empathy and rapport allows you to tailor your approach, anticipate objections, and drive sales. By prioritizing these three elements—Product, Process, and People—you establish a solid foundation for sales success.

Throughout my years in business, I've often encountered issues related to one or more of these three segments. There were times when our products were excellent, but we faced major breakdowns within the team or encountered difficulties in our processes, such as online software affecting our sales. Other times, it seemed like our products were on-trend, and our processes were smooth, but the team required more support. It's a cyclical process, and there will always be room for improvement in one of these areas. Understanding that these three pain points will consistently be present allows you to identify where to invest more time as you grow. Some days, it may focus on your team, while others focus on product growth or refining processes like shipping.

People

My grandfather Ray was a carpet salesman from the 1960s to the 1980s. Ray was known for his ability to make friends anywhere and develop relationships. He knew that a phone number or business card in your Rolodex could be a potential lifetime of sales. For my younger readers, a Rolodex was a set of cards in a box or on a circular, rotating file device that stores contact information for all your leads, like name, phone number, address, and maybe details about their previous conversations. If you were working in the mid-1900s, you would take your Rolodex or leads from job to job and maintain an excellent verbal or working relationship, resulting in a steady income and an incentive for the company to retain you for employment. This is a tried and true format for success in the sales industry. In the 60s-80s, my great-grandmother Edith maintained a relationship of quality service with her salon clients, which allowed for a steady flow of customers regardless of Edith's location. My other great-grandmother Gladys relied on her real estate connections in the 1960s and 70s to garner referrals for new buyers and sellers. Today, that vast Rolodex of connections or leads translates to your followers on social media. In the 1990s and 2000s, the Rolodex morphed into your email list. Today, your growing list of social media followers has become another source for leads that could grow your email list. If you are building a network of potential leads and recruits, the connections you make and maintain in person or online will be critical to your success. Networking and understanding that you are now in the "People Business" makes our job unique and rewarding.

For the remainder of your career, having contact information and knowing the personal details of your customers and leads will be your superpowers. It is easy to assume those connections are solid until time and distance prove they are not. If you were part of the MySpace generation, you would

15

remember the great migration to Facebook. If you have ever had Facebook hacked, you can relate to the tedious task of contacting all of your friends' lists to warn them and then re-friending them with your new account. If you are part of the younger generation, you understand what it is like to have all your followers, friends, and contacts spread across 15 apps, but only a few of the apps can sync together, or they can only sync with your cell phone contact list. If managed correctly, you can amass a large following on your active social media platforms to develop a contact list of potential leads and loyal customers. This customer list will allow you to find connections anywhere, especially since new social media platforms launch almost yearly.

You can personalize your messages and conversations when you know your leads—for example, using their nickname or picking up a previous conversation right where you left off. These techniques help build trust, which is crucial in sales since people prefer buying from someone they know and trust. Every piece of contact info you get could lead to a sale, so having the correct details means you can reach out quickly and keep the conversation going. An important tactic used to maintain relationships or gently push for sales is the follow-up. You can't follow up effectively if you have the wrong contact details or only appear to contact your leads when you want a sale. By seeing how your interactions with leads go, you can figure out what works and what doesn't. This experience helps you adjust your strategies and recommend products or programs your customers may want.

You need a contact list when you are starting. Let's get to work immediately on one. From the people on your list, you can add friends on social media platforms or mail out samples. Set measurable goals to see this list expand as you grow and provide consistent service.

Collecting Quality Contact Information Digitally

In 2014, Google launched a drag-and-drop style free application called Google Forms. This free tool has been excellent for creating forms that are easy to convert into a spreadsheet. Since its inception, we have seen newer versions launch with different graphics, formatting, or options, but they all have the same organizational purpose. Those in the industry know that if a person can quickly and effectively fill out a form, you will get great information on people wanting to learn more about your business. It simplifies the lead information collection process, increases accuracy, enables immediate submission, facilitates data organization, and integrates with other tools to enhance overall efficiency and effectiveness in converting event attendees into potential customers.

In the case of in-person events, attendees often have limited time and attention, with various activities vying for their interest. A quick and straightforward form allows them to provide information efficiently without detracting from their overall event experience. Traditional methods of collecting information, such as paper forms or manual data entry, can be cumbersome and time-consuming for attendees and you. A digital form eliminates these barriers by offering a streamlined process that attendees can complete on smartphones or tablets with a few taps.

Digital forms minimize the risk of errors commonly associated with handwritten forms or manual data entry. By providing clear fields and prompts, you increase the likelihood of receiving accurate and complete information from attendees, ensuring that your sales team has reliable data to work with. With a digital form, attendees can submit their information instantly, allowing you to capture leads in real time. This immediate feedback enables your sales team to follow up promptly while the event is still fresh in attendees' minds, increasing the likelihood of converting leads into customers.

Digital forms automatically organize and store the information collected in a centralized location, such as a Google Sheets spreadsheet or a Customer Relationship Management or CRM system. This centralized database makes it easy for your sales team to access and manage leads, track interactions, and analyze data to inform future marketing strategies. Digital forms can integrate seamlessly with other event management and marketing tools, such as text or email marketing platforms. This integration streamlines workflows, allowing you to automate tasks like sending follow-up and promotional emails or assigning leads to specific sales representatives.

As a real business, you deserve the accuracy, automation, and time-saving benefits of learning to use these tools to your advantage. We will go over the steps in Google Forms, but feel free to use whatever application, service, or software you feel comfortable with. Make sure they protect your data and don't use it to spam or target your potential leads.

Here's a 5-step checklist for creating a Google Form to collect customer information at an event:

1. **Define Your Objectives:** Before creating the form, clearly define the information you want to collect from attendees. The basics should include name, mailing, email address, and phone number. You can also add checkboxes to have them opt into texts or emails. Understanding your objectives will help you structure the form effectively.

2. **Design the Form:** Open Google Forms and start designing your form. Please keep it simple and easy to navigate for users. Add relevant fields for the information you want to collect. Use a mix of text fields, multiple-choice questions, drop-down menus, and checkboxes as needed. You can add questions regarding information about products, parties, or joining. You can add a section to tell me where we met. If you want to send out samples from your company, you can add questions about allergies or preferences in scent. Include instructions or descriptions for each field to guide users on what information to provide. Customize the design of the form to match your branding or theme, if applicable.

3. **Optimize for Mobile:** Ensure your form is mobile-friendly; attendees may fill it out on their smartphones or tablets. Test the form on different devices to ensure it's easy to use and displays correctly.

4. **Set Up Notifications:** Configure the form to send email notifications whenever someone submits their information. This allows you to follow up with leads promptly. You can also set up automated responses to thank attendees for filling out the form and provide them with additional information about your products or services.

5. **Privacy and Compliance:** Include a brief privacy statement or disclaimer at the beginning of the form, outlining how you'll use the

information collected and assuring attendees of their data's security. If applicable, Ensure your form complies with relevant data protection regulations, such as the General Data Protection Regulation(GDPR) or California Consumer Privacy Act(CCPA). Only collect the information necessary for your purposes and obtain consent where required.

Once you've completed these steps, preview the form to ensure everything looks correct, and then share it with users or attendees at your event. Many graphic design sites offer free QR Code generators that you can use to create signage with the form link, or you can have the form open and ready on a tablet. Encourage participation by highlighting the benefits of providing their information and making it easy for them to access the form. Finally, monitor responses and promptly follow up with leads to maximize the effectiveness of your event marketing efforts.

After the event, you can have Google convert the form information into a spreadsheet so that you can move that info to your customer contact list. You can use the spreadsheet to invite people to your customer social media groups, text service, or email lists.

Using I AM bubbles to Brainstorm Connections.

You will inevitably have a moment while compiling your customer list where you forget you have ever met a single person and blank out with panic. It happens to all of us at some point while in business. You have connections around you; they may be woven tightly into your unique interests. Let me prove it:

1. Start with a piece of blank paper and put the words "I AM" in a small circle in the center of the page.
2. Draw a line, then another circle that branches off and says ME in the center. Next, a branch and bubble that says Spouse/GF/BF. Another circle if you have kids (one for each if you have more than one). Another

bubble from the center circle with. Each branch is for work, school, associations, hobbies, and interests. You are starting to create a wheel-type formation with circles branching off the circle in the middle.

3. Then, next to each circle, get specific about the circles that connect you. For example, because of my kid, I know what DIY crafts and Anime are. Because of my other kid, I have learned all about Dungeons & Dragons, robotics, and board games. Each of those circles has opened me up to groups of people with whom I can talk about those interests or bring my products for sharing.

4. Look at the bubbles for overlapping trends, such as interests, connections, or locations. You can also use the bubbles to find friend groups you didn't even recognize you were growing.

This chart is a visual that shows you all of your social connections in a bubble map. It is like a family tree of interests, references, social circles, and groups that can help you create a group of customers, join FB groups, book parties, and even grow a super strong Frontline without saturating a circle with spam. Use this bubble chart to confirm that you have added everyone you connect with to your customer list. As you build up your frontline, some on your team may have crossovers, but no one will ever be exactly like you!

From these bubbles, you can start to create a system of connecting with people in your network. One of the biggest fears of the friends or family of a person joining a direct sales company is someone becoming a one-dimensional robot only able to talk about sales. If you bounce from bubble to bubble with connecting, you can nurture relationships and common interests without over-saturating your connections.

When spending time with people, pay attention to who unites people in each bubble; these friends tend to have already built a network that trusts them and can be a great addition to your network. This friend plans birthdays and get-togethers and may already host parties with direct sales companies for their friends. Set a goal to add one person from each bubble! By having a Frontline in your team from each bubble of your interests, your team can sell to all your circles simultaneously. If you ever end up with every group covered, you can pick up a new interest or hobby and reach a whole new group! This opportunity leaves you room to grow as a person and brand and still have access to all the groups!

Creating a Quality Customer Contact List

Now that we have created a form and crafted a brainstorm of bubbles, we are ready to compile this info in one place. Even if there are five people on this list, gathering the information in one place is a significant accomplishment.

1. Start with any spreadsheet software option you are comfortable with. I like Numbers and Excel for different reasons. Go with what makes you most comfortable. There are many YouTube videos if you are starting from scratch. Save it using a name that is VERY easy to find.
2. Next, let's organize the information we may already have from order histories or contact forms from events. A full business contact will include a Full Name (complete & up-to-date), Mailing Address, Email Address, and Phone Number, so those should also be the titles at the top of your spreadsheet. Later in this chapter, we will use this list for a Google form.
3. Depending on the banking company you are working with, some have options to export or download the list of people who have placed orders from you, or maybe you have it on a service like Paypal or Square you use for vendor events.
4. Enter any contacts on your phone that have expressed interest in your new adventure. These could be friends, family, acquaintances, people you met at a networking event, or coworkers.
5. After you have added the contact information, look for people who are missing pieces of information and reach out to them. I would also like to confirm my other details when I do this so that the entire listing is up to date.

Using This Information Responsibly

Trust in sales starts with providing contact information, which can be used for samples or team membership. It's essential to use this information with good intentions and avoid spam. Staying compliant with rules about collecting contact information shows respect for customers' privacy and keeps businesses legitimate. As a secret keeper, scouting great deals, and trusted advisor, avoid making customers feel guilt or pressure to buy. Pay attention to legal responsibilities when collecting contact information.

How do I pick a leader to join?

People often ask how you pick a sponsor in direct sales. Many join a family member purely because they are the first they have found that are with that brand. Some participate with a friend; later, a family member joins, and things get awkward at dinner, or people have trouble picking between friends.

Here is my official stance on this, and you can completely ignore it if you must: choose a company you love and a leader you can grow with. The one thing I will never say is that your leader dictates your success. You can pick the most successful person, but it does not work out. You can choose the most inexperienced and build something massive. The only component in both situations is you; you must be willing to do the work to be successful either way. Pick the problem that you think will help you grow the best.

That being said, things happen. Most people stay with a direct sales company for about three years, but we had many with us back and forth in our teams for almost a decade. Can you picture how different your life is from a decade ago? We have had teams have life situations come up and have to end their time with us but want to return later; you can do that with most companies. Most companies have great systems for the common situation of someone not loving who they joined with. Call your customer service when things present themselves and ask about your options. Most programs have a window before you can sign up under a new leader in the same company.

3

Getting On Board

Taking the plunge into the dynamic world of direct sales is like entering a land teeming with possibilities. It's where hard work and calculated steps combine with an ambitious mindset to attain success. I still have the same mixture of anxiety and excitement that accompanied my early days of this journey when I think back on them. I was able to use my creativity and solve problems at every turn, from excitedly opening my first starter kit to figuring out how to start my business.

In this chapter, I'll walk you through all the necessary steps to start direct sales. We will also examine doable strategies to increase your income, such as utilizing corporate incentives and cultivating a devoted clientele.

Getting Started

I purchased my bright pink starter kit on November 19, 2013. When it arrived, I opened the information pamphlet in the kit and set my eyes on selling to the first level in the Jump Start program. Next, I created a Facebook event with friends and sent samples to each person to try for the first time. Unfortunately, most items I sent out spilled or failed to arrive. I started to post information about each product at the event, asking those who got the samples in one piece to share testimonials. The first order on my website came from a friend. I was halfway to the first goal. People were buying! Soon after, more orders came in, and I hit my first goal. I closed the party and earned the 15-day reward points to cover more business supplies and some product credits! I also learned I could give my customers product credits as a thank you to help earn more business rewards. Then I wouldn't need to spend more money and could profit from the sales!

Then, it was time to focus on the next goal in the first 30 days and add one new teammate. I had a plan for getting the sales but not one for adding a teammate. Since this was difficult, I decided to focus on that first! As people started to order, I thanked them at the Facebook event! Little did I know I was showing people that my business was growing in credibility and trust. I had a few friends start to ask questions about the starter kit, and I was a bit unprepared, so I returned to the welcome packet in the kit to answer their questions.

On December 1, my company launched a fantastic training program that opened my eyes to a new way of approaching direct sales. Most of my team had never participated in Direct Sales, so we were all worried that we didn't know how to sell. The training we received made team building and sales a little easier and made people feel more confident that they could learn how. Thanks to our new training, customers and recruits quickly emerged from the woodwork. I often had not even considered pitching the product or company to them because I never thought they would be looking for the opportunity!

The first person to join my team was "Tara" (Name changed to protect the awesome). I can still picture the staircase I was staring at, praying she would say yes the first time I asked her to join my team; SHE DID! She had more experience with direct sales parties than I did, so I was able to learn from her. She also built connections while leading one of the military spouse groups. I had already seen her leadership skills, so I was ecstatic to have her be the first to join my team. She helped me achieve the scariest part of my goal for my first month: ONE new teammate. Now, I had to focus on sales again. At this point, I was more intimidated by the team-building side of this business, so I decided that it needed to be my main focus. I would add a teammate, then focus on some sales, then add a teammate, then go back to sales. Like I was weaving my front-line team a strong backbone.

On the way home from a grocery store in Missouri, I met "May." She seemed frustrated about finances when I met her. I had only enough cash to buy a cup of mashed potatoes, yet she listened to me talk about my company after I gave her a bundle of samples to pamper herself after a hard day at work at the Deli counter. After she joined our team, I focused the entire team on ranking up to the first level of the pay plan. In the first moments as a team, I learned that pushing small sales goals together can empower everyone! The point was to not focus on the rank advancement that would only help me but to work together so we all could celebrate. Pushing myself to hit sales goals helped me get more rewards, but seeing us all earn the rewards encouraged us all to feel like superheroes. Teamwork.

At that point, I started to feel like I had a rhythm for the team, focused on a team goal, and crushed it together. As the leader, I would ensure we all did a training video on the team page when someone had a breakthrough or shared resources. We all worked together, and our families started to see the successes in our financial gains. Goals started to become fun to set and were continually rewarding to crush. There was always a reward! I would set up a weekly party link, sell the first level of the party rewards, redeem the rewards, and start over again the following week. This was a steady paycheck I could earn from my couch after the kids went to bed.

During the first 90 days of my business, I learned so much about myself, but the most significant lessons came from those around me. I knew teammates could come from anywhere; people always watch how you are doing first, so show enthusiasm, not fear. If you tell people you are doing great, some will judge, but more will be curious. Focus on those interested and teach them how to do everything you are doing to succeed. Do not gate-keep your working ideas; share them with your team, and you will all succeed. If the team spends time bonding over not more than sales, they can move a mountain because of the mutual support. Every win becomes a team win. We celebrate together.

Step 1: Onboarding Your Business

To start your journey with a Direct Sales company, locate your website. Most modern companies provide access to a back-office dashboard immediately after you submit your application and purchase a starter kit. Logging in and promptly setting up your account is crucial. While waiting for your kit to arrive, consider seeking onboarding training to familiarize yourself with the products and programs. Look for tutorials on finding your website link, where customers can place orders, and your join link, which you share for others to join your team.

Next, find a copy of the company's Policies and procedures or Terms and conditions. These documents outline expectations, rules for partnership, and unclear terms. Familiarizing yourself with these guidelines is vital for understanding how to operate as a company representative.

The second resource to explore is the welcome packet provided by the company. This packet typically includes a welcome letter, details of the compensation plan, incentives for your first sixty or ninety days, instructions for accessing your Back Office, and contact information for customer support. Reading this packet thoroughly can provide valuable insights for starting your business firm.

Another valuable resource is the host program or party link section. Host programs offer rewards for events where customers place orders under a specific link, often earning the host free product credit or free shipping. Setting up a party or event with guidance from your sponsor can help you maximize rewards as you begin marketing your business.

Lastly, locate a digital catalog or online/mobile app showcasing the products you sell. This resource allows you to share product information and images with potential customers before your products arrive, saving on postage costs. Sharing a digital catalog is a cost-effective way to reach your contact list.

Utilizing the incentives and resources provided by the company, such as the 90-day jump-start program, can help you set achievable sales and team-building goals. By combining these programs with commissions, host credits, and other bonuses, you can maximize your return on investment and establish a consistent business growth strategy.

Step 2: Understanding a compensation plan.

Reading a standard sales compensation plan involves understanding its structure, components, and critical terms. Here's a breakdown of the basics for sales commissions, team bonuses, and rank advancement requirements, as well as what to look out for in terms of potential violations from the Federal Trade Commission (FTC):

Sales Commissions:

- **How You Get Paid**: This part explains how much money you make when you sell stuff. It could be a percentage of what you sell or a set amount for each sale.
- **Commission Tiers or Bonuses**: Some plans pay more if you sell a lot. For example, you might get a bonus for selling more than a certain amount.

Team Pay:

- **Earning Together**: If you work with a team, this part explains how your team's success affects your paycheck. You might get bonuses or a share of what the team makes.
- **Teammates and Sponsors**: When someone joins your team, they're your teammate, not just a recruit. Your sponsor is the person who brought you into the team.
- **Group Volume (GV)**: This is the total sales volume of your entire team. It includes your own sales volume plus the sales volumes of everyone you've recruited and everyone they've recruited.
- **Levels and Legs**: In some plans, you might earn commissions based on how many levels deep your team goes. A level is like a step down from you; a leg is a branch of your team that grows under someone else.

Rank Advancements:

- **Moving Up**: To get promoted, you must meet specific goals, like selling a certain amount or leading your teammates to promote. You might need to maintain these goals for a particular period, like a few months or a year.
- **Performance Metrics:** Specific measurements to determine whether you're doing well enough to get promoted. They could be sales targets, customer satisfaction scores, or how many leaders you promote.
- **Qualification Periods**: You might need to maintain certain goals for a specific period to qualify for a promotion. This period could be a few months or longer.
- **Breakaway and Generation**: When promoted, you might "break away" from your sponsor's team. This means your sales no longer count towards their group volume. Instead, they count towards yours. Each breakaway creates a new generation in your team structure.

Potential Red Flags:

- **Watch Out for Scams**: Be cautious if the plan seems too focused on recruiting others rather than selling products. It might not be legit if it promises quick wealth without actual evidence.
- **Misleading Claims**: A plan that promises unrealistic incomes or quick riches without proof could break FTC rules.
- **Retail Sales Required**: Legit companies need you to sell to genuine customers, not recruit more sellers. Plans that skip this could be shady.
- **Stacking and Pyramid Schemes**: Stacking happens when consultants recruit others and place them all under one person in their downline instead of spreading them out. This can manipulate the compensation plan unfairly. Pyramid schemes focus more on recruiting new members than selling actual products, which is illegal.

Always make sure the plan follows the rules to avoid legal problems. If you're unsure, ask someone you trust or get legal advice.

Step 3: Gather your links and make them easily shareable.

One of the challenges faced when launching a direct sales business is the need to share numerous individual links. From promoting your website for purchases to your join link for potential team members, along with various social and informational links, it can quickly become overwhelming. To simplify this process, we'll create a single link with multiple buttons to important pages, making sharing effortless and efficient.

To achieve this, you can utilize websites like Linktree or Stan. These platforms offer drag-and-drop style website generators where you can easily add links and customize them according to your preferences. Best of all, you can use these services for free or premium upgrades for additional features. As you progress, you may consider purchasing a domain link using your name or brand, further enhancing your professional image.

By consolidating all your essential links into a single location, you make it easier for yourself to remember, manage, and simplify the sharing process for you and your audience. This approach reduces confusion and minimizes the risk of errors when dealing with multiple individual links. With just one link, users can access all relevant pages or resources seamlessly, enhancing their overall experience and increasing engagement with your business.

Step 4: Bringing the Customer List to Life

In a previous section, you gathered valuable information about individuals interested in your business, including their name, address, email, and phone number. It's time to leverage all these communication channels to connect effectively with your customer base. Equipped with information, enthusiasm, and product samples, let's bring your customer list to life.

Firstly, let's prioritize reaching out via mail. Crafting a set of samples from your starter kit products along with essential information about your brand, top-selling products, host program, and joining options is critical. Consider presenting this information in a pamphlet, printable, or graphic highlighting your sales funnel's main points. Keep it concise to avoid overwhelming your recipients. Please include the link created in step 2 for them to place orders and find answers to frequently asked questions.

Additionally, consider adding a personal touch with a handwritten thank-you card. This gesture should be cost-effective, akin to the price of a cup of coffee. Once prepared, send out these mailings promptly.

Next, focus on utilizing social media platforms to connect with your audience. Ensure you connect with individuals from your customer contact list on your preferred social media channels. Start promoting your business by posting engaging content, such as a video showcasing the unboxing of your starter kit. If friends are not on your contact list yet, have a Google form ready to gather their addresses for future mailings. You can also create a Facebook group or other social links to promote your business while adhering to sales promotion rules. Later, you can integrate these accounts into your drag-and-drop website or emails for streamlined communication.

Lastly, utilize email, text messaging, and in-person interactions to further engage with your audience. Develop a compelling email campaign using the link mentioned earlier and send it to your customer contact list, announcing your new partnership with the direct sales company. For text messaging, consider utilizing services like Project Broadcast or Remind.com to create and send announcement graphics with the link to your recipients. Additionally, follow up with local contacts to arrange in-person meetings, allowing them to see your products firsthand.

Leveraging various communication channels can help you establish strong connections with your customer base and confidently kickstart your direct sales business.

Step 5: Determining How Much You Can Sell as a Short-Term Goal

Before aiming high, let's start by setting a goal, whether it's for the first level of your company's Jump Start program or your first month in direct sales. Many companies offer scaled rewards systems for customer orders, free shipping, or host rewards. As a beginner in sales, it's beneficial to base your goals on the company's current promotions. These promotions can incentivize customers without spending money out of your pocket.

You can apply the following formula to determine how many orders you'll need to reach your initial goal:

For Beginners: Your total sales goal ÷ the sales promotion price, is the number of people you need to reach that goal.

For example, if your sales goal is $200 and a customer needs to spend $50 to qualify for free shipping, you'll need four orders of $50 each to hit your sales goal. You can then create a drawing for the first four people to place an order on your website or reach out directly to people on your customer list until you've secured all four orders.

For Seasoned Reps: Here's a formula to determine your order average after six months or a year in business:

Your total sales since starting ÷ the number of orders you've had since starting = your order average.

For example, if you've made $250 in sales since starting and have had five orders, then your order average is $50. You can use this order average to set goals for growing to a higher average or maintaining that average.

For More Experienced Sellers: If you're an experienced seller, you can personalize this formula based on your order average. It would look like this:

Your total sales goal for the year ÷ your sales order average = the number of people you need to hit that goal yearly. Divide that number by 12 to get your monthly goal.

For example, if you want to sell $12,000 yearly and your sales order average is $50, you'll need 240 orders annually. Dividing this by 12 gives you a monthly goal of 20 orders. You can create an incentive program for the first 20 people who place an order over your average in a month or divide it weekly to ensure you have five orders each week to stay on track throughout the month.

These formulas can help you set achievable sales goals based on your level of experience and the current promotions offered by your company. Adjust them as needed to fit your specific situation and goals.

Step 6: Beware the Do's & Don'ts of Beginner Sales

Building real connections with your customers is essential when starting your sales journey. Instead of just trying to make quick sales, take the time to get to know them and understand what they need. Listen carefully to what they say, ask questions, and offer helpful advice tailored to their situation. Providing valuable information and tips for your products can show that you care about their well-being and can help you earn their trust.

One thing to avoid is being too pushy or aggressive when trying to make a sale. Nobody likes feeling pressured into buying something they're not sure about. Instead, aim to educate and guide your customers so they can make informed decisions independently. Also, don't forget to follow up with potential leads and existing customers. Keeping in touch shows that you value their business and can help you close more sales in the long run.

It's also important to be honest and transparent about what your products can do. Making big promises that you can't deliver on will only hurt your reputation in the long run. When you get feedback from customers, whether good or bad, listen to what they say. Feedback can help you improve your products and services, showing customers that you value their opinions.

Lastly, make sure you're prepared for every sales interaction. Know your products inside and out, know industry trends, and anticipate common customer questions. Being prepared will help you answer questions confidently and build customer trust. Following these tips and avoiding common pitfalls can set you up for success in your sales journey. Always be prepared for a potential client interaction.

4

Selling The Dream

I t's common to feel confused about how to sell when signing up with a direct sales company. Questions like "Am I selling when I create a graphic? Am I selling when I message everyone I know? Am I selling when I invest in large quantities of stock hoping to sell it all?" are valid because many companies provide training that lacks clarity. To find answers for myself, I had to draw from my past experiences in retail or restaurants to realize that unless I defined sales as the actual moment when a product is sold to a customer, I'd fall into the same trap that many direct sales representatives encounter daily: the blurred line between sales and marketing.

Sales vs Marketing, the never-ending fight

When things get cloudy, let's define our terms for clarity:

- Sales are operations and activities involved in promoting and selling goods or services.
- Marketing is the process or technique of promoting, selling, and distributing a product or service.

This debate of sales and marketing has gone on for decades. I picture sales as when I talk to you and sell you an item, but when I think of marketing, it is when I post about it on my social media. I am not expecting that to be a targeted sales conversation. Without marketing to inform your customers of your excellent products and their value, many sales would not happen. But if you only go person-to-person to sell, you will never attract enough people to your brand to get off the ground. This situation is how you end up back to selling pizza to only your friends and family, and everyone gets heartburn.

Let's delve into a fundamental sales concept known as the sales funnel, which has been a crucial element of marketing strategy for more than a century. Developed by E St. Elmo Lewis in 1898, it's considered the first formal marketing theory. This tool serves as a blueprint for various aspects of your business, including designing your vendor booth, crafting your party script, arranging the layout of a pop-up store, or even structuring your website. We'll utilize the sales funnel to assist you in team building and gaining a deeper understanding of your customers.

Stage 1: What is (insert product or business name)?

Let's say you are starting from scratch with a potential lead! In this stage, a person doesn't know who you are or recognize your logo or products. That is why many experts call this the Awareness stage; they know you exist! This interaction will be their first encounter with the idea and possibly your brand. They don't know what they are missing but aren't missing it. When a potential lead first learns about your product or brand, they must also be educated about it. This can be accomplished using innovative marketing tools or through an in-person experience.

Some in Direct Sales look for ground floor, new ideas, or new companies to promote a brand that has not already gained brand recognition or saturation. The upside to this type of opportunity is that you may have lots of room for growth and not have a ton of representatives locally to compete with you while you get off the ground floor. A downside is that this stage requires someone who wants and has time to pound the pavement. This person will have to recognize that much of that pavement will be focused purely on marketing and gaining brand recognition.

It is important to note that the Awareness stage is not a linear but cyclical process. In the direct sales industry, I have seen companies launch "new" product collections that are available elsewhere and have already saturated the market. Products related to CBD, skincare technology, makeup, nutrition, or patches, to name a few. They do so because the product is profitable, which means it can also be profitable to the sales rep. Upon release of these product collections, many seasoned sales reps realize that the Awareness stage is starting over for them and their customers. It is understood that to be successful, they must return to customers with knowledge, excitement, and potential benefits of their innovative products. Thereby creating awareness and hype with customers about the new product and why they need it before the sales rep even considers pitching the sale. The time spent educating can be frustrating but will be rewarding when your leads and customers find that "thing" they absolutely must have.

Many direct sales companies tend to release new product lines on a seasonal basis, but some do not. That means you may be able to become well-versed in the Awareness stage process. Sales reps who do not experience this trend often should find ways to remind themselves of what it feels like to be in this stage. I would drive through a part of town that I did not frequent. I would focus on businesses in the area to observe their success, what kind of foot traffic they could see, the longevity of that business since my last drive, and whether or not I hear about those businesses after leaving the area. This simple act reinvigorates my drive to market and publicly use the products I sell. Taking the opportunity to show bystanders the packaging and its purpose, maybe even offering to share or sample the product with a stranger. While immersing others around you in your branding, it must be understood that there will always be people who feel you don't have what they need. Understanding that fact will help you tailor your marketing strategy to the needs of new people coming into view and plan how you want to help them!

Stage 2: Have you tried (insert product or business name)?

In this step, people recognize that your brand, product, and business exist but do not have personal experience yet. They may have seen a few ads, maybe a friend tried it, and perhaps they saw it at an event. This is when potential customers become interested in sampling your product or service, welcoming you into the Interest stage. Now is the time for them to express interest in what you may have to offer.

Some may join a company with a recognized brand when determining which direct sales company to represent. Doing so allows them to skip the Awareness stage with consumers familiar with the brand and jump right to trying it out. As a new rep, they can hold launch parties and immediately hit the ground running without explaining the company's background, what product genre is being sold, or what service is being provided. As a potential sales rep aspiring to join a Direct Sales company during the Interest stage, you may want to look for a company that offers a starter kit and a good selection of products to sample or share upon arrival.

At this point, it must be said that when you have products to showcase, you must do so. Re-enter the Awareness stage to inform your leads or past customers of your new endeavor or products. Sparking excitement will pull people back into the Interest stage, where you can offer samples or invite them to an event to try out the products. Encourage potential customers to share or invite friends and family to generate new leads. Showcasing the product or service you offer through social media will allow those following your posts to see that "thing" they may need. Social media marketing has become a staple and the lifeblood of convenient sales opportunities for the direct sales rep. However, using social media as a sole means of marketing can be frustrating, especially if you keep posting and are not getting much attention. That's why we diversify our methods to continually bring people through the Awareness and Interest stages, both from home and whenever you leave the house. It is essential to recognize that every time you leave the house, there is an opportunity to showcase and share your products or services with others. To accomplish this, you must *ALWAYS* have something on your person for people to try or experience, navigating them through your brand's Awareness and Interest stages. You want something easy to share without needing a sales pitch or presentation. If social media is the only means of marketing, try posting an offer of 5-10 sample packets consistently on your social media weekly or monthly so potential customers can claim and try them. Product exclusivity and limited supply can create urgency for free samples.

As you create a team of sales reps, it is essential to regularly remind them and guide them through the Awareness and Interest stages of what you are offering. This tactic will keep them interested and teach them to do the same for their teams and customers. When I need to remind my team of this stage, I tell teammates to open a new product from our company that they have not yet tried. Be sure to pay attention and take notes about how they are picking items to try. Is it the smell, the taste, the feel? Did they read the label? What is drawing them in? Finally, invite them to use the item. While doing so, I have them attempt to see the world through the eyes of someone trying something from their business for the first time. I note the impact their senses have on what is drawing each teammate towards a particular product. From there, I can use this information to create a marketing strategy that includes this in my brand's messaging.

Stage 3: Did they purchase (insert product or business name)?

OK, they know you exist, have tried your products, and decided to purchase! You have now entered the Purchase stage. Your potential customer is making the decision that they want to buy your stuff or service. They are paying more attention to what you offer, including deals and options, so that they can get the most out of every dollar. This is where your knowledge and business acumen come into play. Knowing precisely what you can offer and provide will give your new customer options and allow you to "upsell" through bundling products/services, offering rewards/benefits, and discounts.

If you are fortunate enough to be in a position where you see a need for a product or service but no one to provide it, you might consider joining a direct sales company that allows you to skip the first two stages upfront. A company that already has a loyal following and/or where you have been loyal. A business where potential customers, you know, could benefit from your initiative to sell what they already have enjoyed in the past. Jumping into an opportunity such as this will allow you to immediately send potential customers your consultant link without the effort of initially navigating through the Awareness and Interest stages of the sales funnel. This will enable your new customers to find the products/services they are familiar with while also creating an opportunity to educate them about new products and services since their last purchase, repeating the cyclical nature of the sales funnel.

The Purchase stage can also be a great place to find new teammates. Loyal customers who love the product/service and would like to receive them at a discount while benefiting from sharing with their network of potential customers. It has been most beneficial in my product sales experience to search for a company that offers the best starter kit. It may be easier to transition potential teammates into joining if they have immediate access to many products without breaking the bank. I often see successful transitions when your potential teammate is offered a special deal, incentive, or limited edition product upon joining your team to generate excitement. It can be rewarding to transition from a customer or host to a consultant on your team.

From the customer's perspective, at the Purchase stage, they are looking for a discount, added value, or the feeling that their money was well spent. Considering this aspect, throughout your marketing strategy and execution, it is essential to feature sales, deals, bundling, fundraising, and benefits to increase your chances of connecting with people considering purchasing. There are many marketing tactics to experiment with, but keeping things simple will prevent you from being overwhelmed. For example, adding product/service graphics showcasing what you offer on social media can help people connect and get the word out about your business. Direct sales have the flexibility to empower customers with the ability to host product parties. Like the Tupperware parties of old, you and your hosts can give options to potential customers that also double as a host incentive program. These programs have the added benefit of helping hosts decide if they want to move forward and become consultants or remain loyal customers and receive product/service discounts.

Stage 4: Have they shared (insert product or business name)?

Many assume a sale is the end of the sales funnel; if so, they have lied to themselves and given up WAY too soon. Word-of-mouth marketing has always paid out significantly and consistently regarding return on investment (ROI). It all comes down to people looking out for people instead of corporations telling people what they want. To that point, we are back at TRUST. We have entered the Sharing stage of the sales funnel, which, in my opinion, is the most inspiring part of direct sales. So stay focused!

For those of us already in direct sales, the Sharing stage is when customers beg you for a party to ensure their friends and family hear all about your offerings and the company! Just kidding, that rarely happens, so let's talk about reality. Many see this stage as hosting a party, meeting with potential customers for coffee after kid dropoff, or networking at an event. But more likely than not, this is the moment you may never see when they buy a gift from your website for a family member during the holidays or share your link. It is that critical moment when it goes from a personal purchase to a group experience. This is the stage where you discover your brand, and all your hard work is not just a product or service to buy but an experience to share.

Those of us who happen to be looking to join a company at the Sharing stage have already benefited from the aspects of the Purchase stage. Now, there is the added enjoyment of sharing. You may want to join around a gift-giving holiday, in the Spring or Fall. You may wish to share trend-forward, visually stunning products or services you benefited from. Whatever the reason, you already recognize that word-of-mouth marketing and product sharing are significant in generating excitement around a product/service. For word-of-mouth marketing and sharing to work, you want the start of your business and the products you plan to sell to fit naturally with your audience and your authenticity. Some people are uncomfortable sharing online or in person, but focusing on sharing will enable you to reach more people like parent groups, hobbyists, and networking event participants outside your usual circle.

After joining and getting comfortable sharing for years, some reps have trouble picturing that first moment when you might still be shy and worried about giving products as gifts or sharing with a friend. I like to have them remember the last time they tried something new but focus on the feeling of HAVING TO SHARE with someone nearby. I asked them to picture taking a bite of something and immediately deciding the person next to them was also required to taste it. I have seen almost every person do this to their friends or family in a smell-goods store. That is sharing! You are so passionate about your experience that you cannot even consider that someone would not feel the same way, and you refuse to keep them from living without it. I have seen this with skincare, food, music, and makeup. The product becomes an experience that becomes so infectious and exciting that you run around and pull people into your moment. It becomes an instinct to find things worth sharing. This is when you start to see your influence over friends. One buys the coffee and posts; everyone buys the coffee and posts. One buys the lipstick; we all buy the lipstick. That is how they feel when they love your brand and products. They cannot contain themselves. That is the same feeling you want people to have when they see your brand messaging and are ready to share it with others.

Stage 5: Will they sell (insert product or business name)?

Let's discuss the next step in this funnel, the Join stage. This is a critical and often expensive stage that many get into. You find this fantastic product or service; it is easy to share, and suddenly, you see the money. After all, your friends are buying it up because you told them it was incredible!! The stage we enter is when sharing is not enough for you; it is when you want to earn a commission from sharing this product and turn it into a business. You can see a need in the market(demand) and feel the product or service can fulfill their needs while being profitable(supply).

At this stage, a Direct Sales customer considering joining your company will ask you more about things behind the curtain. They exhibit a different pace and purpose to the questions they start to ask. In Direct Sales, a conversation about a starter kit can go in a few different directions, but it is your job to decipher what is being asked. Some may state they are looking for additional income to pay a bill. Someone probing about your sales' consistency and what kind of consistency to expect may be showing interest. A person may ask how long you have worked with a particular company. They want to know how long it will take to reach an equivalent level and make a substantial income. The most apparent ask is whether or not your company provides training on how to work this business and product education. This person COULD build a business for life if given the correct resources.

Your Closest Exit

When discussing sales funnels, it's crucial to understand that individuals can exit at any stage. They might glimpse your logo or products and decide it's not for them. They could try your offerings once and then disappear. Some might purchase from you once but never return. The key is recognizing when someone isn't interested and letting them go, focusing instead on those keen to learn more. This is why eighty percent of your sales will come from loyal customers, with only twenty percent from new customers. You can't force someone to move through the funnel if they're uninterested. It's like giving a timeshare pitch to a group waiting to be rewarded with a gift card or chasing window shoppers down like a pushy salesperson in a mall. While pressure tactics might lead to a sale, they won't foster a healthy sales relationship in the long run and could lead to avoidance.

Offer them a slice of cake.

Much like offering cake all day, selling involves continuously reaching out to potential customers and engaging with them through touch points. Think of touch points as moments of interaction with a potential customer. Just like offering them a slice of cake at that moment, you create an opportunity to connect and build a relationship. Potential customers may not want cake then, but the simple offering will leave a lasting impression. The consistency of offering that cake at different touch points may eventually result in a "yes." It is that moment when your customer has a need, and you present a product or service for that need at the right place and time.

First, it's essential to understand that sales isn't just about someone saying yes to you. It's perfectly OK for people to say no because it doesn't set you back further than when you started the conversation. For instance, if you offer someone cake and they decline, move on and ask someone else. Don't take it personally.

Moreover, rejection in sales isn't personal. Just because someone declines your offer doesn't mean it's a reflection of you or your product. Take, for example, someone declining cake because they're gluten intolerant. It's not about you; it's about their dietary restrictions. Understand the reason behind the rejection and move forward.

Persistence is critical in sales, but there's a fine line between being persistent and overly pushy. You want to continue reaching out and making your offer, but you must also respect people's boundaries. And remember, just because someone says no today doesn't mean they won't say yes in the future. Keep offering your product or service, and you may find success down the line.

In essence, your job in sales is to keep offering the cake—engaging with potential customers, building relationships, and providing value. Focus on the process rather than fixating on individual responses. By doing so, you'll navigate the sales journey with confidence and resilience.

Building awareness with touch points.

As we've explored the various sales funnel stages, from generating awareness to converting leads into customers, it's crucial to recognize the importance of engaging with potential customers at every stage of their journey. Each stage has touchpoints that present an opportunity to build relationships, provide value, and drive sales.

A touch point refers to any instance or point of interaction between a customer and a business throughout the consumer's journey. These interactions can happen across various channels, including in-person engagements, online platforms, social media, email, phone calls, and more. Touch points are pivotal in shaping the customer experience and influencing perceptions, attitudes, and behaviors toward a brand or product. Touchpoints can also include website visits, social media engagement, email correspondence, customer support interactions, physical store visits, product demonstrations, advertising efforts, and post-purchase interactions like onboarding and follow-up support. Effective management and optimization of touch points are critical for businesses to craft positive and seamless customer experiences, foster relationships, and drive satisfaction and loyalty.

Regarding touch points, I feel the need to mention sending samples and managing shipping from home. It has been my experience that sending samples allows potential customers to experience the quality and benefits of your products firsthand, helping to build trust and confidence in your brand. Much like offering that slice of cake, you may be sending the product or delivering the service they most need to be fulfilled when your sample arrives. Meanwhile, setting up business shipping from home lets you fulfill orders efficiently and promptly deliver products to your customers. This has been most helpful during the holiday season when smaller direct sales companies are swamped with high shipping demands.

Throughout the sales funnel stages, you must identify critical touch points where you can connect with potential customers and provide value. Each touch point offers an opportunity to engage with customers, address their needs, and guide them through purchasing. This is where your customer list is most important and comes into play again. When engaging in touch points, noting what is happening in their lives may be beneficial, such as the potential customers' needs or issues, positive family moments and accomplishments, or plans. These items will help navigate future touchpoint interactions that will foster trust, build relationships, and maybe even generate a sale because you can provide something they need. By effectively leveraging touch points and incorporating marketing strategies, such as sending samples and managing shipping from home, you can create a seamless and personalized customer experience. Ultimately, this will increase brand loyalty, higher conversion rates, and long-term success for your business.

As we delve deeper into these topics, we'll explore practical strategies and best practices for maximizing the impact of each touch point and driving results throughout the sales funnel. From sending samples to managing shipping logistics, you'll be equipped with the tools and insights you need to succeed in today's competitive marketplace.

Here's a breakdown of shared touchpoints many use from the initial meeting to closing a sale:

Initial Meeting/Introduction: You won't get a second chance at a first impression! The first impression is crucial, regardless of whether the interaction is in-person or online. Your meeting or interaction could be planned or by happenstance, but how you present yourself in that moment will determine how that person views you as an individual.

Networking Follow-up: After the initial meeting, follow up with a friendly email or message expressing your pleasure in meeting them and suggesting ways to collaborate or connect further.

Social Media Engagement: Connect with them on social media platforms like LinkedIn, X, or Facebook. Engage with their posts, share relevant content, and build rapport.

Email Newsletter Subscription: If applicable, encourage them to subscribe to your email newsletter for updates, insights, and special offers related to your product or service. There are a plethora of low-cost automated services you can utilize to make this process easier. Services like Mailchimp, Brevo, and Omnisend, to name a few, enable you to create and schedule automated emails.

Personalized Email Outreach: Send targeted emails based on their interests and needs, providing valuable information or resources related to your product or service.

Content Marketing: Share relevant blog posts, articles, videos, or other content that demonstrates your expertise and addresses their pain points or interests.

Webinars or Workshops: Invite them to participate in webinars or workshops where they can learn more about your industry, product, or service in a more interactive setting.

Product Demonstrations: Offer personalized product demonstrations or consultations to showcase the features and benefits of your offering and address any questions or concerns they may have.

Recommendation: Provide a detailed recommendation outlining the specific solutions you can offer to address their needs, along with pricing and terms.

Follow-up Calls or Meetings: Schedule follow-up calls or meetings to discuss the recommendation, answer any remaining questions, and address any objections they may have.

Negotiation and Customization: Negotiate terms, discuss customization options, and tailor the offering to suit their needs better if necessary.

Closing the Sale: Once all concerns have been addressed and both parties are satisfied with the terms, close the sale by finalizing the order, processing the payment, and confirming the deal.

Post-Sale Follow-up: After the sale, follow up to ensure a smooth onboarding process if they join, provide additional support or resources as needed, and express appreciation for their business.

Customer Feedback and Reviews: Encourage customers to provide feedback and reviews on their experience with your product or service, which can help build credibility and attract future customers.

Referral Program: Invite satisfied customers to participate in a referral program where they can refer others to your business in exchange for rewards or incentives.

By strategically engaging with potential customers across these touchpoints, you can effectively nurture relationships and guide them through the sales process toward a successful close.

Sampling

Taking a more in-depth look, sampling out products can be a powerful tool in your sales arsenal. Sampling will allow potential customers to experience the quality and benefits of your offerings firsthand. When sampling products or services, it's essential to have a clear strategy to maximize their impact and drive sales.

Firstly, identify which products you want to sample based on their popularity, unique selling points, or relevance to your target audience. Consider offering a variety of samples to cater to different preferences and needs. Choose items likely to resonate with your audience, like skincare products, health supplements, or home goods.

Next, determine the best approach for distributing samples. This could involve hosting sampling events at local fairs, markets, or community gatherings or offering samples during one-on-one interactions with potential customers. Additionally, consider incorporating samples into your social media or email marketing efforts to reach a broader audience.

When distributing samples, provide clear instructions on how to use the product and highlight its key benefits. Consider including a promotional flyer or business card with each sample, directing recipients to your website or social media pages for more information or to make a purchase.

Follow up with recipients using touch points that follow after they've tried the sample to gather feedback and answer any questions they may have.

This allows you to further engage with potential customers and address any concerns they may have, ultimately increasing the likelihood of a sale.

Overall, sampling out products can be an effective way to generate interest, build brand awareness, and ultimately drive sales. By carefully selecting products, strategically distributing samples, and following up with recipients, you can leverage sampling to grow your business and attract new customers.

Following up after sending samples is critical to maintaining momentum and nurturing relationships with potential customers. Here are some touch points that a person can utilize for effective follow-up:

1. **Email Follow-up**: Send a personalized email a few days after sending the samples to inquire if they have received them and if they have had a chance to try them out. Express interest in their feedback and offer to address any questions or concerns they may have.

2. **Phone Call**: A friendly phone call can be an effective way to follow up after sending samples. It allows for direct communication and provides an opportunity to discuss their experience with the samples, answer any questions, and gauge their level of interest.

3. **Personalized Thank You Note**: Send a handwritten thank-you note expressing appreciation for their time and consideration in trying the samples. Personal touches like this can leave a lasting impression and demonstrate your commitment to customer satisfaction.

4. **Social Media Engagement**: Engage with them on social media platforms like LinkedIn, X, Facebook, or Instagram. Like, comment on, or share their posts about the samples they received, and initiate conversations to keep the interaction going.

5. **Follow-up Survey**: Send a brief survey to gather feedback on their experience with the samples. Ask specific questions about what they liked, what could be improved, and whether they would consider purchasing the whole product.

6. **Offer Additional Information or Resources**: Provide additional information related to the samples they received. Information such as product specifications, usage tips, or customer testimonials will build

credibility in your knowledge while increasing trust in the product or service. This can also help reinforce the value proposition and address any lingering doubts.

7. **Invite to Discuss Further**: Invite them to schedule a follow-up meeting or call to discuss their thoughts on the samples in more detail. Use this opportunity to delve deeper into their needs and preferences and explore how your product or service can meet them.

8. **Special Promotion or Discount**: Offer a special promotion or discount on their first purchase as a token of appreciation for trying out the samples. This can incentivize them to take the next step towards making a purchase.

9. **Check-in Email**: Send a brief check-in email a couple of weeks after the initial follow-up to see if they have any additional questions or are ready to purchase. Keep the lines of communication open and be responsive to their needs.

10. **Referral Request**: If they have a positive experience with the samples, ask if they know anyone interested in trying them. Please encourage them to refer friends or colleagues to expand your reach and generate more leads.

By utilizing these touch points for follow-up after sending samples, you can keep the conversation going, address any concerns, and ultimately move closer to converting potential customers into satisfied buyers.

SETTING UP SHIPPING FROM HOME

Setting up business shipping from home can be a convenient and cost-effective way to fulfill orders and deliver products to your customers. Remember, we are trying to avoid one of the biggest pitfalls of direct sales by reducing our costs and increasing our ROI. With the right tools and resources, you can streamline the shipping process and ensure timely delivery of your products.

First, depending on your shipping needs and preferences, you must decide what service you want to use for printing labels. From there, you can create accounts with shipping carriers like USPS, UPS, FedEx, or DHL. Pirate Ship is my favorite label printing service because it has no additional fees, prints labels on my home printer, and discounts carrier rates.

Once you've chosen your shipping carriers, you must invest in shipping supplies such as boxes, envelopes, packing materials, and labels. As of today, USPS has many shipping supplies, such as Flat-rate shipping boxes or envelopes, on its website for free. Other retailers like Amazon, Vistaprint, and Uline have materials you can pick or design to match your branding. Consider purchasing these items in bulk to save money and ensure you have an adequate supply to fulfill orders efficiently.

Next, set up a designated shipping area in your home where you can package and process orders. Ensure this area is well organized and equipped with all the necessary supplies and equipment, including a printer for printing shipping labels. You would be surprised how often the printer is overlooked.

If you run your shop or website, consider using shipping software or online platforms like Shopify that integrate with your e-commerce platform or website to streamline the shipping process further. These tools can automate tasks such as printing shipping labels, calculating shipping costs, and tracking orders, saving time and effort.

Regarding shipping rates, research the pricing options your chosen carriers offer and determine the most cost-effective solution for your business. Consider package size, weight, and destination when calculating shipping costs for your customers.

Finally, communicate shipping policies and expectations to your customers, including estimated delivery times, tracking information, and applicable shipping fees. Transparent and reliable shipping services can help build customer trust and loyalty and ensure a positive shopping experience.

By following these steps and implementing best practices, you can set up business shipping from home efficiently and effectively. This will allow you to quickly fulfill orders and deliver products to your customers.

After shipping an order, it's essential to maintain communication and provide a positive post-purchase experience. Here are some touch points after sending an order:

1. **Order Confirmation Email**: Immediately after placing the order, send a confirmation email that includes order details, estimated delivery date, and any relevant tracking information.
2. **Shipping Notification**: Once the order has been shipped, send a shipping notification email or SMS with tracking details so that the customer can monitor the delivery progress.
3. **Delivery Confirmation**: Follow up with a delivery confirmation email or message once the order has been delivered. Include a thank-you note and invite them to share their feedback on the purchasing experience.
4. **Post-Purchase Survey**: Send a post-purchase survey to gather feedback on the ordering process, shipping experience, and product satisfaction. Use this feedback to improve your services and offerings.
5. **Product Usage Tips**: Provide helpful tips or instructions on how to use the purchased product effectively. This can enhance the customer's experience and ensure they get the most value from their purchase.
6. **Cross-selling or Upselling**: Recommend complementary products or accessories that may enhance the customer's purchase. This can be included in the delivery confirmation email or as a follow-up communication.
7. **Discount for Future Purchase**: Offer a discount or promotional code for their next purchase as a gesture of appreciation for their business. This can encourage repeat purchases and foster customer loyalty.
8. **Customer Support Availability**: Communicate your customer support contact information and availability in case the customer has any questions, concerns, or issues with their order.
9. **Request for Product Review**: Encourage the customer to leave a review or testimonial about their experience with the product and the purchasing process. Positive reviews can help build trust and credibility for your brand.
10. **Follow-Up Email Series**: Implement a follow-up email series to check

in with the customer after they've had time to use the product. Provide additional tips, answer common questions, and offer support if needed.

11. **Membership or Loyalty Program Invitation**: If applicable, invite the customer to join your loyalty program or membership club, where they can receive exclusive benefits, discounts, or rewards for their continued patronage.

Implementing these touch points after shipping an order can enhance the overall customer experience, encourage repeat purchases, and foster long-term relationships with your customers.

In conclusion, it's essential to understand the difference between selling and marketing when it comes to selling through direct sales. We've discussed the sales funnel, a customer's journey from knowing nothing about your product to buying it. Each step along the way has its challenges and opportunities.

By sampling and handling shipping from home, we can ensure we're reaching out to potential customers most effectively. It's all about building relationships and ensuring people trust us and our products. As we keep working on our strategies and finding new ways to connect with customers, let's focus on providing value and giving people the best experience possible. Together, we can keep growing and finding success in direct sales.

5

Building A Brand

Establishing your brand in direct sales presents a unique challenge: self-acceptance. Central to this journey is understanding and embracing your true identity and recognizing that your persona deserves acknowledgment and appreciation. You must realize you control what you convey; authenticity can magnetize a devoted following.

Before fully defining ourselves, we must recognize that external influences such as parents, friends, and societal norms often shape our perceptions. Overcoming these rooted opinions can feel overwhelming, especially when confronted with statements like, "Why aren't you more like…" or "You have to fit this mold to succeed." The objective is to free yourself from these constraints and embrace your authentic self and imperfections. These imperfections are what make your brand relatable and genuine.

So, how do you translate your authenticity into a brand? It begins with staying true to yourself and integrating genuine aspects into your brand identity. You don't have to conform to every expectation. You must live authentically and naturally align your products or services with your audience's interests. Being disingenuous about your motives for sharing products can breed distrust. Your audience craves authenticity, seeking to understand why they should heed your advice and anticipate your next move. Be prepared to evolve and vocalize your passions while maintaining enthusiasm throughout your sales journey.

Cupcakes

My introduction to personal branding developed unexpectedly amidst the chill of a North Dakota winter, where I hastily established a nonprofit business fueled by my passion for baking. It began modestly, crafting treats for my husband, Dave, to take to work. However, the spark ignited in 2010 with the inception of Cupcakes for Haiti following the devastating earthquake. Crafting both traditional and inventive flavors, I secured permission to set up a stand in the Delta Vacations break room, quickly selling out and donating the proceeds to the United Nations Food Program.

The momentum was undeniable as requests poured in, prompting the launch of my cupcake venture upon leaving Delta Vacations. With a bustling calendar of orders and an innovative approach to flavor combinations, my creations captured attention and hearts across town. Every mishap, like turning buttercream into whimsical ice cream sundaes, only fueled my creativity and dedication.

In early 2011, a newfound sense of purpose led me to design a Valentine's Day initiative benefiting families impacted by domestic violence. What began as a simple idea became a community-driven endeavor, culminating in assembling 33 baskets filled with essentials and heartfelt gestures.

As opportunities to make a difference presented themselves, I refused to accept limitations. When funding for the Deployed Spouse group dwindled, I rallied resources and baked tirelessly to comfort and support military families. The outpouring of generosity and solidarity was infectious, inspiring others to join the cause.

The defining moment that arrived in 2011 was when Minot, ND, faced unprecedented flooding. Undeterred, our community rallied, mobilizing resources and support in a remarkable display of service before self. From coordinating relief efforts to comforting National Guard members, the experience underscored the transformative power of collective or community action.

Amidst the chaos, my brand emerged as a creator of delicious treats and a catalyst for positive change. Customers didn't just buy cupcakes and see me as the Cupcake lady; they invested in a vision of community empowerment and compassion. This ethos laid the foundation for my transition into direct sales, prompting reflection on what resonated with my audience and how to foster a sense of belonging and purpose.

Reflecting on the journey, it becomes clear that branding isn't just about products; it's about forging meaningful connections and fostering a community united by shared values and aspirations. Here's how you can harness that same spirit to propel your direct sales business forward.

Components of a Brand

When you search for the term "brand" online, you'll find it defined as a product manufactured by a specific company under a particular name. But branding encompasses more than just a product—it's about promoting your business through advertising and distinctive design. These elements shape how people perceive you, your values, your message, what you offer, and your story.

Your brand is essentially how individuals view and interact with your business. Ready for an awkward third person? Take, for example, my name, Sasha Sweder. It may evoke thoughts of the person and the brand associated with my business. While Sasha Sweder, the individual, may be engaged in everyday tasks like caring for children or enjoying leisure time, Sasha Sweder, the brand, embodies a determined, late-night entrepreneur fueled by coffee or a martini, striving to inspire others and build an empire. This differentiation between the person and the brand is pivotal. My brand projects a polished image—I can barely say that with a straight face—reflecting someone who adeptly manages household chores and exudes focused determination. Establishing such a brand identity is critical, and we'll explore this further in the upcoming challenge.

In this context, the focus is not solely on the products you sell but on you—the individual behind your brand. Consider a hair salon; as the owner, you are the face of the business, recognized for your values and principles. You play a pivotal role in shaping the environment where your brand thrives. From designing the storefront to assembling a team aligned with your brand's objectives, you set the tone. Your team's services, characterized by content and character, craft an experience that mirrors your brand's essence. Your products complement this brand experience, allowing your community to immerse themselves. In our analogy, you embody the blank white walls of the salon—your spirit should infuse the foundation and walls so deeply that replicating what you've built becomes inconceivable.

Creating a solid brand involves several key components that shape how your audience perceives your business. Here are some of the most essential elements:

1. **Brand Identity:** This encompasses the visual elements of your brand, including your logo, colors, typography, and overall design aesthetic. Consistency across these elements helps establish brand recognition and reinforces your brand's personality.
2. **Brand Personality:** Your brand should have a unique personality that resonates with your target audience. Are you playful and fun or serious and professional? Defining your brand's personality helps humanize your business and makes it more relatable to consumers.
3. **Brand Values:** Your brand values are the guiding principles that inform everything you do as a business. They reflect what you stand for and what matters most to you. Communicating your values helps build trust and loyalty with your audience.
4. **Brand Voice:** Your brand voice is the tone and style of communication you use in your messaging, whether on your website, social media, or in advertising. Consistency in your brand voice helps reinforce your brand identity and creates a cohesive brand experience.
5. **Brand Story:** Every brand has a story; sharing yours can help forge emotional connections with your audience. Your brand story should communicate who you are, why you do what you do, and what sets you apart from the competition.
6. **Brand Experience:** Customers' overall experience with your brand— from their first interaction with your website to their post-purchase

support—is crucial for building brand loyalty. Creating positive experiences at every touch point helps strengthen your brand reputation and encourages repeat business.

7. **Brand Promise:** Brand promise is your commitment to your customers and the value they can expect from your products or services. Delivering on this promise consistently is essential to build trust and credibility.

8. **Brand Positioning** refers to positioning your brand in the marketplace relative to your competitors. Understanding your target audience and identifying what sets you apart can help you carve out a unique position that resonates with your customers.

By paying attention to these components and ensuring they align cohesively, you can create a solid and memorable brand that effectively communicates your value proposition and connects with your audience.

Branding Can Take Your Audience on a Journey with You

Reflecting on my online presence, I've often found it a tapestry of diverse interests. From my culinary adventures to my experiences as a military spouse and later delving into direct sales and the enchanting world of Disney, each chapter of my journey has shaped my online persona. Yet, despite recognizing that I am the common thread weaving through these varied interests, I struggled to effectively engage with each audience simultaneously and highlight their shared connections.

In this branding challenge, you'll discover how to bridge these gaps and foster connections among your diverse audience members. For instance, one segment of your audience may be avid movie enthusiasts; addressing a specific need or desire requires tying their love of the cinema with the relevance of your products or services. By authentically sharing various aspects of your life and interests, you can connect with individuals across different social circles and lifestyles, creating a sense of community that transcends individual interests.

Initially, your audience may engage with your content based on a single topic they associate with you. However, as you authentically share your experiences and expertise across different areas, they'll gradually become acquainted with your multifaceted persona. Over time, this fosters trust and credibility as your audience recognizes your authenticity and passion across various subjects.

Consistently and genuinely sharing across diverse topics allows you to broaden your audience's understanding of your interests while establishing credibility across various areas of expertise. Ultimately, you want your brand to catalyze connection and bring together individuals from different backgrounds and interests under a shared umbrella of authenticity and shared experiences.

Creating A Personal or Team Brand

Step 1. Decide your brand messaging and your team branding.

What are the key messages you want to communicate about your brand? What are the key messages you want to share about your team brand? Every teammate or customer should be aware of your brand attributes.

This step is essential to establishing clear and consistent communication about your brand across all touchpoints and stages of the sales funnel. Start by identifying the core messages that define your brand identity. These messages should encapsulate your brand's values, mission, vision, and unique selling propositions. The Unique Selling Proposition (USP), also known as a Unique Selling Point, is a distinctive feature or characteristic of a product, service, or brand that sets it apart from competitors in the marketplace. It is a clear and compelling statement that communicates the unique benefits or advantages your brand offers customers. The USP answers the question, "Why should customers choose this product or brand over others?" by highlighting what makes it unique, valuable, or superior. Effective USPs resonate with the target audience's needs, desires, or pain points, often serving as the focal point of marketing campaigns to differentiate their offerings. USPs are meant to drive consumer interest and loyalty. Consider what sets your brand apart from competitors and what you want customers to associate with your brand.

Once you've defined your key brand messages for you and your team, ensure everyone is familiar with them, especially teammates. Consistent messaging helps reinforce your brand identity and ensures everyone in your organization is aligned with your brand's goals and values.

To effectively communicate your brand messaging, consider developing internal training materials, workshops, or regular team meetings focused on brand awareness. Encourage the team to embody the brand values during online and offline customer interactions. By fostering a shared understanding of your brand messaging among your team, you can create a unified brand experience that resonates with your target audience and builds trust and loyalty over time.

Step 2: Create a "voice" that reflects your personal and team branding.

Developing a distinctive voice for your personal and team branding is essential for consistently conveying your brand's personality and values across all communication channels. This voice should be evident in all written content, including your website, social media posts, marketing materials, emails, etc.

Consider each brand's characteristics and the impression you want to leave on your audience. Is your brand friendly and approachable? Is your brand in line with your target demographic? In any case, your voice should be conversational, engaging, and warm. If your brand projects a sense of sophistication and elegance, your voice might be more formal and refined.

The key is to align your voice with your brand's identity and target audience. Imagine each brand as a person – what qualities would they possess? How would they communicate with others? By defining your brand's voice, you can create a consistent and authentic tone that resonates with your audience and strengthens your brand identity.

Authenticity is the most critical aspect of establishing your brand's voice. Your voice should reflect your brand identity and remain true to your values and personality. It's about being genuine and relatable to your audience while effectively communicating your message.

Step 3: Get a great logo.

Logo design, while only one aspect of branding, often serves as the focal point of branding initiatives. Ensure your logo or brand mark is prominently featured across various platforms. Research and utilize reputable logo design apps like Canva, TailorBrands, Fiveer, and Makr, selecting the most updated options. These apps typically offer cost-effective solutions, allowing for multiple iterations without significant expense. Look for transparent PNG images for versatility in light, clear, and dark backgrounds. Educate yourself on different types of logos, such as word marks, brand marks, letter marks, or iconic logos, and personalize your design while maintaining simplicity.

For Direct Sales (DS) professionals: design logos for your name and website (suitable for social media), your name and the site name (without the website URL, ideal for personalizing emails, signing documents, letterheads, and business cards), your team's name (in alignment with the overall business branding), and the blog name (without the .com extension, for use in site headers or informational sections).

Step 4: Create a tagline.

Crafting a compelling tagline is essential for encapsulating the essence of your brand in a concise and memorable statement. Your tagline should resonate with your audience, conveying the unique value proposition of your brand in a meaningful way.

Start by brainstorming phrases or slogans that reflect your brand's key attributes and values. Consider what sets your brand apart from competitors and what message you want to convey to your target audience. Your tagline should be memorable, catchy, and authentic to your brand identity.

Reflect on phrases or expressions you frequently use in your communication, whether during videos, presentations, or everyday conversations. These phrases could serve as inspiration for your tagline and contribute to the authenticity of your brand voice.

Once you've generated ideas, refine them to ensure they are concise and powerful. Aim for brevity while still capturing the essence of your brand. Your tagline should leave a lasting impression on your audience and resonate with them emotionally.

Ultimately, your tagline should be a powerful tool for reinforcing your brand identity and effectively communicating your brand's values and personality. It should encapsulate what your brand stands for and evoke a positive response from your audience.

Step 5: Design templates and create brand standards for your marketing materials.

Establishing consistent branding across all marketing materials is essential for reinforcing your brand identity and creating a cohesive brand experience for your audience. Begin by developing templates for various marketing collateral, including social media posts, fliers, brochures, email newsletters, and more.

Ensure all materials for each brand should adhere to the same color scheme, logo placement, and overall look and feel. Consistency is critical to building brand recognition and trust with your audience. Using the same visual elements across all materials reinforces your brand's identity and makes it easier for customers to recognize and engage with your content.

Consider using tools like Canva or other graphic design software to create and customize templates according to your brand standards. These tools allow you to consistently incorporate your brand colors, fonts, and logos across all marketing materials.

Additionally, establish brand standards that outline guidelines for using colors, fonts, logos, and imagery. This ensures that anyone creating marketing materials for your brand follows the same design principles and maintains consistency. Include color codes, preferred fonts, logo placement, and sizing guidelines.

Refer to the Pinterest boards created in the previous chapter for inspiration and visual guidance as you develop your brand standards and templates. Visualizing your branding elements can help you make informed decisions and ensure that your marketing materials accurately reflect your brand identity and values.

The goal is to create visually appealing and consistent marketing materials that effectively communicate your brand message and resonate with your target audience. Adhering to brand standards and utilizing templates can streamline your marketing efforts and maintain a cohesive brand image across all channels.

Step 6. Integrate your brand.

Branding should permeate every facet of your business operations, encompassing visual elements and how you conduct yourself and interact with others. Consider how your brand is represented in every touch point of your business, from customer interactions to internal communications.

Start by ensuring consistency in how your brand is presented across different channels and mediums. This includes elements such as your company logo, color scheme, and messaging, which should be reflected in everything from your website and marketing materials to your email signatures and social media profiles.

Beyond visual branding, consider how your brand is experienced in personal interactions. Train your team to embody your brand values and maintain consistency in communication and behavior. This includes how they answer phone calls, interact with customers, and even what they wear during sales calls or client meetings.

Personal branding is also essential. Consider how your appearance and demeanor contribute to your brand image. For example, you might choose clothing that reflects your brand's personality and values, ensuring that you feel confident and aligned with your brand identity when meeting new people or attending business events.

Integrating your brand into every aspect of your business creates a cohesive and memorable brand experience for your customers and stakeholders. Consistency in branding fosters trust and credibility, helping to solidify your brand's identity and differentiate your business in the marketplace.

Step 7: Be consistent.

Customers rely on your brand promise to guide their expectations of your products or services. Your brand promise should be ingrained in every aspect of your business, reflecting your core values and what you stand for. It's not only about visual elements like color schemes; it's about creating an authentic and consistent experience or product.

Think of your brand promise as the foundation of your products, services, or experiences. It should be something you can confidently deliver without overpromising or stretching yourself too thin. Your brand promise must align with your business's capabilities and strengths.

Your brand promise should evoke a sense of trust and reliability, making customers feel confident in choosing your brand over competitors. Whether it's exceptional customer service, high-quality products, or a unique value proposition, your brand promise should be something that sets you apart and reflects what you claim to provide.

Consistency is critical to delivering on your brand promise and promoting your brand overall. Ensure that every interaction, from marketing campaigns to customer service interactions, reinforces your brand's values and commitment to fulfilling its promise. Consistency builds trust and loyalty among your team members and your customers.

While delivering on your brand promise may require effort and dedication, it's absolutely imperative for your business's long-term success. Utilizing tools such as auto-scheduling for social media or customer relationship management systems will help you stay consistent and effectively deliver your brand promise. Investing the time and energy into fulfilling your brand promise will ultimately pay off in customer satisfaction, loyalty, and business success.

6

Marketing Your Magical Self

et's begin our exploration of the 4 Ps of marketing by imagining the construction of a house. While neither you nor I may have wielded a hammer to build a home, this analogy offers a tangible framework to understand the intricacies of marketing strategy. Imagine that this house represents your marketing strategy as a business owner, particularly one involved in direct sales.

As a direct sales representative, establishing your branding online is essential for several reasons. Personal branding is the foundation upon which you build credibility and trust within your industry. By showcasing your expertise, experience, and personality online, you cultivate a sense of authenticity that resonates with your audience, making them more receptive to your suggestions. In a crowded marketplace, personal branding sets you apart from your peers, allowing you to highlight your unique characteristics and showcase why customers should choose to engage with you. Whether it's your specialized knowledge, distinct personality, or the added value you provide beyond the products themselves, personal branding enables you to carve out a niche and distinguish yourself in the minds of consumers.

However, personal branding extends beyond mere self-promotion; it's about nurturing meaningful relationships with your audience. You foster customer trust and loyalty by sharing valuable content, actively engaging with your network, providing personalized recommendations, and boosting repeat sales and referrals.

Moreover, developing your branding online involves engaging with the core marketing principles or the 4 Ps: product, price, placement, and promotion. You learn to tailor your messaging to highlight your products' unique features and benefits, ensuring they resonate with your target audience. Simultaneously, you acquire the skills to price your offerings competitively while maintaining profitability, identify the most effective channels to reach your audience, devise strategies to promote your products, and effectively engage with your network.

By nurturing your brand, you bolster your sales efforts, open doors to new opportunities, and expand your network. Connecting with like-minded individuals, industry experts, and potential customers online creates avenues for growth and collaboration within your business.

Personal branding is a line through which you leverage marketing principles to connect with your audience, drive sales, and ultimately build a thriving business. Through a deep understanding and adept application of these principles, you can unlock the full potential of your products, pricing, placement, and promotions while fostering enduring relationships with your audience.

The 4 Ps of Marketing

I want to introduce you to the 4 Ps. The 4 Ps of marketing, also known as the marketing mix, is a foundational framework that outlines the critical components of a marketing strategy. E. Jerome McCarthy first presented this concept in the 1960s in his book "Basic Marketing: A Managerial Approach." The first focus is the **product.** This refers to a company's goods or services to its customers. It includes aspects such as the product's features, quality, design, branding, and packaging. As a small business owner, understanding your product and its unique selling points is the bedrock for developing a successful marketing strategy. You need to ensure that your product meets the needs and desires of your target market and stands out from competitors. The second focus is **price.** Price refers to the amount customers are willing to pay for your product or service. Setting the right price is a delicate balance between profitability and competitiveness. Factors to consider when determining the price include production costs, competitor pricing, customer-perceived value, and pricing strategies such as skimming penetration or value-based pricing. As a small business owner, pricing your product effectively can help attract customers and maximize revenue.

The third focus is **place.** Place, also known as distribution, refers to the channels and methods used to make the product available to customers. This includes decisions about where to sell the product, such as through retail stores, online platforms, or direct sales, and considerations about distribution logistics, inventory management, and transportation. Understanding your target market and their purchasing habits is essential for selecting the proper distribution channels and ensuring your product is accessible to customers.

The last focus is **promotion.** Promotion encompasses all the activities undertaken to communicate the product's benefits and persuade customers to buy it. This includes advertising, public relations, sales promotions, personal selling, and direct marketing. The promotion aims to create awareness, generate interest, stimulate demand, and drive sales. Developing a cohesive promotional strategy that effectively reaches your target audience can help increase brand visibility, build customer loyalty, and drive revenue growth.

As a direct sales representative, creating your brand outside the company you have joined by applying the 4 Ps of marketing can help you develop a well-rounded marketing strategy. A strategy that will effectively target your desired customers, differentiate your product from competitors, maximize sales and profitability, and ultimately contribute to the long-term success of your business. By carefully considering each element of the marketing mix and how they interact, you can create a cohesive and strategic approach to marketing that aligns with your business goals and objectives.

Products and services - What do you sell?

The product you plan to sell to your network is the cornerstone of your marketing strategy, much like the foundation of a house. It represents a tangible or intangible good that aims to fulfill a specific customer need or demand. Just as a builder meticulously plans each stage of construction, marketers must understand and anticipate the various stages of a product's life cycle, along with their unique challenges.

It's imperative to grasp the problems your product aims to solve. Delve into its benefits, understand all its features, and unearth its unique selling proposition (USP). Moreover, it's essential to identify and comprehend the potential buyers of your product.

What you sell is as important as who buys it, where you are located, how much it costs, and how you present it. If you offer subpar quality, you risk losing the trust you've painstakingly built. Think of it like a hairstylist using cheap products to boost salon profits—customers will notice and lose faith in your brand.

When crafting your product strategy, consider the entire ecosystem around it. Find the perfect fit that aligns with your values and excites you. Just as a chef meticulously designs a menu or a baker selects core items for their display case, focus on what sets your product apart and makes it irresistible to your target audience.

Don't merely sell products; sell dreams. Show your customers the transformative experiences and solutions your product can provide. By doing so, you'll not only attract sales but also cultivate long-term loyalty and trust in your brand.

Price - How much is it?

Price is a critical component of your marketing strategy, akin to selecting the suitable materials for constructing your house. It encompasses the amount the end user is expected to pay for your product, directly influencing its sales. However, pricing isn't solely about the cost of production; it's primarily about the product's perceived value to the customer.

Understanding how your customers perceive the value of your offering is essential. A product may command a higher price than its objective financial value if it effectively delivers meaningful customer benefits or addresses specific needs. Conversely, a product lacking perceived value may require strategic underpricing to entice buyers. Distribution plans, production costs, markups, and competitor pricing also affect the pricing equation.

Consider the balance between affordability and quality. While some customers may have a specific price point, they may be willing to spend more for a bundle offering long-term value or ethical sourcing. For instance, customers may prioritize products from companies that prioritize responsible sourcing, fair labor practices, or environmental sustainability.

Ultimately, the decision to accept your pricing rests with the customer. By carefully aligning your pricing strategy with customer perceptions and needs, you can balance affordability and quality, fostering customer loyalty and driving sales.

Place - Where will you sell it?

Place, also known as the distribution location, is an integral aspect of your marketing strategy, analogous to selecting the perfect location for your house. It pertains to how your product will be provided to customers and encompasses the entire distribution process. Your placement strategy involves evaluating the most suitable media for your product to reach your target audience.

Consider where you set up shop or establish your online presence. Are you creating a vibrant website, shop, or blog, or do you have a physical storefront in your community? Are you regularly at local events like farmers' markets, or do you host recurring meetings at a nearby coffee shop? Essentially, where you position yourself is where customers will find you. Understanding the preferences and habits of your target market is pivotal to your success. For instance, if your customers frequent local markets and value seasonal ingredients, ensure your presence aligns with those values.

If you've laid the foundation with a great product and priced it competitively, it's time to focus on local engagement and location strategy. Have you contacted other businesses with similar interests, offering mutual support and perhaps shared meeting spaces? Are you hosting community events or after-school specials to attract families? By actively engaging with your community, you strengthen your presence and foster a sense of belonging.

A place can also reference where you can be located virtually. Imagine painting the picture of your business on platforms like Pinterest and Etsy while securing contracts for vendor events or farmers' markets and establishing a consistent presence. Participating in local activities and partnering with complementary businesses or organizations expands your reach and builds a supportive community around your brand. Regular team meetings in familiar locations further solidify your presence and enhance customer trust.

Your place strategy is more than just physical location; it's about creating connections, building relationships, and becoming an integral part of your community. By strategically positioning yourself where your customers are, you increase visibility, drive engagement, and ultimately foster long-term success for your business.

Promotion - How will you sell it?

Promotion embodies the culmination of all the communication strategies and techniques to showcase your products or services. Much like designing the interior of your house to create a welcoming atmosphere, you need to promote your offerings in a way that is appealing to consumers. This means advertising, sales promotions, special offers, public relations, and other methods to spread the word about your business. However, ensuring that the channels and methods you choose align with your product, pricing strategy, and target audience is essential.

Consider how you'll reach your audience: Do they primarily engage locally or online? How will you announce your business's launch? Will you host a grand opening event or rely on digital invitations and word-of-mouth referrals? For companies with a diverse customer base, like mine, it's essential to maintain a solid online presence to serve remote customers while fostering a sense of connection.

Social media is pivotal in my marketing strategy, allowing me to engage with customers regardless of location. Just as you carefully design the interior of your house, I'm crafting a digital space that reflects my brand's personality and values. From posting daily specials and local volunteer opportunities to sharing tips and promoting community events, every promotion aspect is geared toward creating a welcoming and engaging environment for customers.

By applying the principles of the marketing mix—product, price, place, and promotion—you can bring your business to life and create a compelling experience for your customers. Just as building a house requires careful planning and attention to detail, developing a successful marketing strategy involves understanding your target audience, positioning your product effectively, engaging with your community, and promoting your brand authentically. By following these principles, you can establish a strong foundation for your business and create long-lasting connections with your customers.

7

Social Media Marketing

Social media marketing is often simplified to posting attractive images and catchy captions. However, it's far more than aesthetics—it's about understanding algorithms and leveraging statistics to connect with your audience effectively. Successful social media marketing isn't just about pretty pictures; it's about crafting content that resonates with your target audience and drives engagement.

Consider this: when you post a photo with a captivating caption, you're not just sharing an image but initiating a conversation and fostering a sense of community. Every aspect of your post—from the background color to the product placement—plays a vital role in capturing attention and encouraging interaction. It's a meticulous process that requires attention to detail and understanding your audience's preferences.

Your brand doesn't start with your direct sales business; it reflects who you are and your accumulated experiences over time. Every new connection you make, every skill you acquire, and every personal interest you pursue contributes to the essence of your brand. Much like an influencer seamlessly integrates a new product line into their content, you can organically incorporate your business into social interactions.

Yet, many individuals hesitate to promote their business on social media, fearing the potential scrutiny and judgment from their existing network. It's a daunting prospect in a society where validation often comes as likes and follows. However, it would be best to recognize that you control how and when your brand interacts with others. Embracing this control empowers you to confidently share your business with your social circle, knowing that some may embrace it while others may not—a natural part of building a brand and establishing your presence in the marketplace.

Social Media Feels Like The High School Cafeteria

Let's reframe the scenario: envision a bustling high school cafeteria, each table representing a different facet of your life. Your friends occupy these tables, and you're faced with the daunting task of choosing where to sit, feeling the pressure of potential judgment if you don't choose wisely. This sense of unease mirrors the balancing act many feel between their personal life, work obligations, leisure time, and family commitments when promoting their business on social media.

Now, let's reimagine those tables without the friends but filled with topics you're passionate about. You engage with your family on Mondays, eagerly anticipating catching up with loved ones. Tuesdays are dedicated to embracing your work life, perhaps even donning taco-themed attire for Taco Tuesday. Wednesdays are for coffee with mom's friends, indulging in discussions about motherhood. As you share recipes and restaurant reviews with fellow foodies, Thursdays become a culinary adventure. Fridays are event planning days, Saturdays are for self-care, and Sundays offer a well-deserved rest. Each day brings its rhythm, allowing for meaningful interactions without overwhelming yourself or your audience.

Simplifying your approach and creating designated spaces for different aspects of your life can significantly reduce stress and chaos. You shouldn't feel pressured to be constantly present on every social media platform, bombarding your audience with relentless sales pitches. Instead, focus on delivering content that empowers, educates, and energizes your followers.

Authenticity is key. It's okay to share the highs and lows of life as long as you provide value and support to your audience. Whether you're discussing challenging topics or offering solutions, aim to inspire rather than demoralize.

People gravitate towards positivity and authenticity, seeking content that resonates with their values and interests.

Your social media content should reflect your brand's overarching themes. Whether you're sharing cat videos or engaging in political discussions, ensure that your content aligns with your brand identity and provides value to your followers.

Navigating social media can feel overwhelming, akin to moving into a new apartment with fresh carpet and a blank canvas. You may stumble, make mistakes, and experiment with different approaches. Embrace this journey enthusiastically, but recognize the importance of refining your strategy and presenting your best self to your audience.

It's time to roll up your sleeves, tidy up your social media presence, and present a polished image to the world. Like preparing for a visit from your discerning parent and their friends, take pride in delivering your best self on social media.

Old way: In the early days of social media sharing, it was acceptable to approach promotion with a more casual and sometimes unprofessional demeanor. People frequently slapped their logos onto images or quotes, battering their audience with excessive promotional content. Live videos were often unpolished, featuring individuals who may not have put much effort into their appearance or presentation. Direct messages were commonly used to push products or solutions onto unsuspecting recipients, regardless of their relevance or interest. Social media feeds were cluttered with divisive or inappropriate content, lacking cohesion or strategic direction. It was a chaotic and often ineffective approach to building a brand presence online.

New way: Today, there's a growing emphasis on professionalism and strategic planning in social media promotion. Instead of bombarding their audience with constant promotions, businesses focus on providing value and building genuine connections. Live videos are carefully planned and executed, with attention given to content and presentation. Direct messages are used sparingly and thoughtfully, offering personalized recommendations or assistance tailored to the recipient's needs. Social media feeds are curated with purpose, featuring content that aligns with the brand's values and resonates with its target audience. Overall, there's a shift towards more intentional and professional engagement on social media platforms, reflecting a commitment to quality and authenticity in brand representation.

Content over Confusion

In a previous chapter, we introduced the concept of a bubble chart to help you visualize your social circles and interests. Let's focus on how and where your audience wants to hear your voice.

The term "content" can be overwhelming, with numerous resources offering various strategies. Let's simplify: content is the substance that fills the space between memes, cat videos, and quotes unless those are part of your brand, in which case, they become content. To simplify this, let's create a bucket system to clarify your approach.

There are four primary outcomes to consider in content marketing:

1. **To entertain:** Create content with strong emotional appeal, making it highly shareable. Aim to evoke laughter, tears, or any strong reaction from your audience.
2. **To educate:** Offer informative content that broadens your audience's knowledge, making them feel knowledgeable and clever.
3. **To persuade:** Develop content that gradually changes consumer perceptions, focusing on building credibility and trustworthiness.
4. **To convert:** Craft content facilitating rational decision-making, presenting your products or services as the solution to your audience's needs.

Now, let's distinguish again between marketing content and sales content:

- **Marketing content** builds authority and establishes your company's identity within the market. It focuses on educating and persuading your audience.

- **Sales content** aims to communicate urgency and demonstrate the value of your solution. It's about convincing your audience to make a purchase.

To fill these content buckets, consider utilizing various formats:

- **Video:** Platforms like YouTube, Snapchat, Facebook, Instagram stories, and TikTok/Musically.
- **Pictures:** Utilize Instagram and Facebook profiles and platforms like Flickr.
- **Words:** Embrace blogging and article writing to convey your message effectively.

Now that we've simplified the approach and clarified the content buckets, it's time to reflect on who you want to reach and where they're most receptive to your message. Take a moment to pause and revisit the question: Who do you want to talk to, and where do you need to speak to them so they hear you?

Topics of Interest

Now that we've established your branding, let's dive into the interests and topics that resonate with your audience. Maintaining authenticity and avoiding becoming a mere corporate entity devoid of personality is essential to humanizing your brand. Your identity should be the cornerstone of your social media interactions. People seek genuine connections with individuals, not faceless logos.

Think about your life before joining (insert company). What were your hobbies, habits, and passions? Whether running with a club, pottery painting at the YMCA, or attending playdates, reconnect with those activities. Authenticity is vital—straying from your true self can make others perceive you as robotic and disingenuous.

Moving forward, it's essential to be authentic and personal online. Share moments from your life that showcase how you genuinely incorporate your products or services. If you didn't take the photo yourself, reconsider sharing it—your audience wants to see authenticity and real-life usage of products. Discuss how your products fit into your daily routine or share related experiences, such as volunteering or attending events.

Authenticity builds trust. Your audience wants to see how your products or services seamlessly integrate into your life. By sharing personal experiences and interests, you humanize your brand and make it relatable.

As you refine your approach, your interests and connections will naturally blend, creating a cohesive and engaging online presence. For instance, you might discover common ground with acquaintances in unexpected places, like bumping into a PTA friend at the grocery store. These connections deepen your relationships and expand your network.

Moving forward, focus on finding your audience and engaging with them authentically. Utilize hashtags, keywords, captions, and blog posts to connect with like-minded individuals. Stay true to your topics and delete anything irrelevant to maintain consistency.

Find your table.

Identifying where your target audience spends their time online is essential for effective social media promotion.

1. **Social Networking Sites:** Platforms like Facebook, X, and LinkedIn facilitate personal connections and knowledge-sharing. Utilize these platforms to network with customers and teammates, create ads compliant with your policies, and leverage hashtags to connect with like-minded individuals.
2. **Social Review Sites:** Platforms like Yelp, Influenster, and TripAdvisor provide valuable insights through user reviews. Monitor these platforms to understand customer perspectives and learn from other companies' interactions with their customers.
3. **Image-sharing sites:** Platforms like Instagram and Snapchat are ideal for visually engaging content. Encourage users to share images featuring

your products with unique hashtags to inspire and engage your audience.

4. **Video Hosting Sites:** Platforms like YouTube and TikTok offer potent opportunities for video content. Create quality videos, engage with the community, and comment on relevant topics to build your presence.

5. **Community Blogs:** Platforms like Medium and Tumblr provide spaces for sharing thoughts and connecting with readers. To engage your audience, experiment with creating educational, persuasive, and entertaining content.

6. **Discussion Sites:** Platforms like Reddit and Quora foster discussions around various topics. Engage with users in your field, answer questions, and establish yourself as a thought leader.

7. **Sharing Economy Networks:** Platforms like Uber and Airbnb connect individuals with services and resources. Explore these networks to find opportunities for networking and collaboration relevant to your business.

Ensuring consistency across all platforms is necessary for brand recognition and professionalism. Use your branding and business title to secure your profiles and maintain consistency in profile pictures, descriptions, and links across all platforms. Consider using your photo as your profile picture to establish trust and connection with your audience. While professional headshots are ideal, they focus more on authenticity than perfection.

Leveraging Blogging for Enhanced Search Engine Optimization and Branding

Blogging isn't just about sharing stories; it's a strategic tool for boosting your online presence and reinforcing your personal and team branding through effective search engine optimization (SEO) and keyword integration.

In our life journeys, we often encounter vulnerabilities and complexities. By courageously sharing these experiences through blogging, we connect with others and enhance our visibility in online searches. When crafting your blog posts, consider incorporating keywords related to your business, team, and personal branding. These keywords serve as digital signposts, guiding potential customers and team members to your content and reinforcing your brand identity.

Understanding your audience is critical to effective blogging. Identify the individuals who influence your interests and connections—the pillars of your personal and team branding. For instance, if your business revolves around health and wellness products, your blog can explore topics related to holistic living, fitness journeys, and self-care tips. You can attract relevant traffic and strengthen your online presence by aligning your content with your audience's interests and needs.

Embrace vulnerability in your blogging journey. Share your learning experiences, mistakes, and triumphs authentically. This humanizes your brand and fosters trust and connection with your audience. Incorporating personal anecdotes and insights into your blog posts enhances engagement and reinforces your authenticity and credibility as a trusted authority in your niche.

Additionally, blogging allows you to address specific topics and challenges within your industry, positioning yourself as a thought leader and expert. By sharing valuable insights, tips, and solutions, you provide value to your audience and improve your search engine rankings by targeting relevant keywords and topics.

Blogging is a powerful tool for enhancing your SEO, strengthening your personal and team branding, and establishing yourself as a trusted authority in your industry. By strategically incorporating keywords, sharing authentic stories, and providing valuable content, you can attract targeted traffic, engage your audience, and drive growth for your business and team.

Creating a Social Media Marketing Strategy Plan

Step-by-Step Guide: Creating Your Social Media Brand Strategy

1. **Define Your Brand Identity:** We did that in Chapter 5! Identify your unique selling points, values, and mission. Then, determine how you

want to be perceived by your audience.

2. **Know Your Audience:** Research and understand your target demographic by asking questions about your favorite topics that cause your followers to share their opinions. Identify their needs, preferences, and pain points. Tailor your messaging and content to resonate with your audience.

3. **Choose Your Platforms Wisely:** Select social media platforms where your target audience is most active. Find your cafeteria table! Consider the nature of your products. Are they easy to share in pictures, videos, or posts? What type of content do you plan to share?

4. **Create Consistent Branding:** Develop a cohesive visual identity across all platforms. Use consistent colors, fonts, and imagery that align with your brand.

5. **Craft Compelling Content:** Plan a content strategy that aligns with your brand identity in Chapter 5 and resonates with your audience. Create a mix of informative, entertaining, and promotional content. Utilize a variety of formats, such as images, videos, and blog posts.

6. **Engage and Interact:** Foster genuine connections with your audience, as discussed earlier in this chapter, by engaging with their comments, messages, and mentions. I love looking up engagement question ideas on Pinterest! Participate in conversations related to your industry and niche. Encourage user-generated content and testimonials.

7. **Implement SEO Strategies:** Incorporate relevant keywords and hashtags into your posts to improve discoverability with a blog, long posts on FB, or comment sections on review websites. Optimize your profiles with keywords, content captions, or search engines to increase visibility.

8. **Measure and Analyze:** Track critical metrics such as engagement, reach, and conversion rates. Use social media analytics tools to gain insights into the effectiveness of your strategy. Adjust your approach based on data-driven insights to continuously improve your performance.

9. **Stay Authentic and Transparent:** Maintain authenticity in your

interactions and content. Be transparent about your products, services, and business practices. Build trust with your audience by being genuine and honest.

10. **Adapt and Evolve:** Stay informed about the latest trends and changes in social media algorithms. Continuously refine and adapt your strategy based on feedback and market trends. Experiment with new ideas and tactics to keep your brand fresh and relevant.

Following these steps, you can create a comprehensive social media brand strategy that effectively promotes your direct sales business and builds meaningful connections with your audience.

8

Vendor Events

There is no time to explain. Get in; we are going to sell! The following two chapters will bring the sales funnels to life in ways that allow your business to reach customers, connect fast with all the information they need to decide to invest in you without being overwhelmed, and effectively follow up on loose ends. Picture vendor events as the opportunity to hold a pop-up shop for your branding! This is my favorite part of our job! Let's get to work.

Finding Events to Participate In

Finding suitable venues to showcase your products or services in direct sales is pivotal to your success if you decide to sell using the "cash & carry" method. Local vendor events, festivals, and fairs offer an active platform where you can engage with potential customers face-to-face, build relationships, and drive sales. However, not all events are created equal, and it's essential to identify those that align with your brand and target audience. Here's how you can navigate the landscape of local vendor events to maximize your direct sales efforts.

Firstly, research is your greatest ally. Start by compiling a list of upcoming events in your area, utilizing online resources, community bulletin boards, and local event listings. I love to check out social media for events created locally. Look for events that attract a diverse and sizable crowd, ensuring ample foot traffic to maximize your exposure. Consider the demographics of attendees – are they likely to be interested in your products? Events catering to specific interests or demographics can provide a more targeted audience for your products or services.

Secondly, vet the credibility of the event organizers. Reputable organizers prioritize the success of their vendors and maintain clear communication throughout the process from contract to close down. Seek out events with a track record of attracting quality vendors and attendees, which indicates a well-established and respected event within the community. Don't hesitate to contact past vendors for feedback on their experiences and inquire about factors such as attendance numbers, booth fees, and promotional opportunities.

Thirdly, evaluate the cost-benefit ratio. While participation fees are inevitable, weigh them against the potential return on investment. Consider the booth fees and additional expenses such as travel, accommodation, and promotional materials. Calculate your anticipated sales and exposure to determine whether the event aligns with your budget and sales goals. Remember that the value of participating in an event extends beyond immediate sales – it's also about brand visibility in advertising, networking opportunities with other vendors, and fostering long-term customer relationships.

Lastly, prioritize professionalism and presentation. Your booth should serve as a compelling storefront, drawing attendees in and effectively showcasing your products or services. Investing in eye-catching displays, signage, and promotional materials that reflect your brand identity and resonate with your target audience adds to the event's expense. Engage attendees with interactive demonstrations, product samples, and exclusive offers to entice them to learn more and purchase. Ensure that the event provides everything you need to connect with people who will love your brand. Remember, the impression you leave at these events can impact your brand reputation and customer perception.

By strategically selecting and participating in local vendor events, festivals, and fairs, you can amplify your direct sales efforts and unlock new growth opportunities. Approach each event with thorough research, professionalism, and a customer-centric mindset, and watch as your business thrives in the dynamic world of direct sales.

Booking an event.

Once you've found the perfect event to showcase your products or services, it's time to negotiate the nitty-gritty details of contracts and expectations with the event coordinator. Don't let the paperwork overwhelm you—with a bit of savvy and preparation, you can ensure a smooth and mutually beneficial partnership for years in some cases.

First and foremost, understand the terms of the contract. A contract is simply a written agreement that outlines the responsibilities and obligations of both parties – you and the event organizer. Review the contract carefully, paying close attention to critical details such as booth fees, setup and tear-down times, and any promotional opportunities included. If something isn't clear, don't hesitate to ask questions and seek clarification from the organizer.

Set clear expectations from the get-go. Communication is vital to a successful partnership, so don't be afraid to voice your needs and concerns. Discuss logistical details such as booth location, when they will have a schedule of the event prepared, location for entering for set up and break down, seating in the booth, access to electricity, and any specific requirements for your setup. Establishing a clear understanding of what's expected from both parties helps prevent misunderstandings and ensures a smoother experience for everyone involved.

Cover your bases and protect yourself from potential risks. While most event organizers have your best interests at heart, being aware of potential pitfalls is essential. Ensure the contract includes provisions for unforeseen circumstances such as event cancellations, inclement weather, or changes in venue. Consider investing in liability insurance to protect yourself against accidents or damages during the event. It may seem like an extra expense, but it's well worth the peace of mind it provides.

Keep your commitments and fulfill your obligations. Once you've signed on the dotted line, you must honor your agreement and uphold your end of the bargain. Arrive at the event on time, set up your booth professionally, and engage with attendees courteously and enthusiastically. Remember, your reputation as a reliable and trustworthy vendor can go a long way in securing future opportunities and building lasting relationships within the community.

In summary, navigating contracts and expectations at events doesn't have to be daunting. By taking the time to understand the contract terms, communicating effectively with the event organizer, and protecting yourself from potential risks, you can set yourself up for success and make the most of your participation in local vendor events, festivals, and fairs.

Designing Your Vendor Event Booth for Maximum Impact

Designing an effective vendor event booth is crucial for connecting with potential customers, spreading brand awareness, and boosting sales. By applying the basics of the sales funnel to your booth setup, you can guide attendees from first glance to making a purchase.

First, catch people's eyes with attention-grabbing graphics that represent your brand and offerings. Use vibrant colors, striking images, and brief messages to leave a memorable impression. Consider using banners or signs that showcase your brand identity and highlight key features or benefits of your products. You can order these once your branding is created in our previous chapter. I like using the colors from that branding for the tablecloths, accents, and signage. Once assembled, it should look cohesive.

Next, create interest by offering interactive experiences within your booth. Set up "try me" stations where people can sample your products firsthand. Offer exclusive deals to encourage purchases and posters that explain the benefits of joining your company or hosting events.

Once you've captured their interest, focus on building desire. Use persuasive techniques like customer testimonials or success stories to build trust and credibility. Highlight the perks of joining your company, such as discounts or extra income opportunities, and use visuals like before-and-after photos to showcase your product's effectiveness.

Finally, make it easy for attendees to take action. Place your checkout area prominently and display starter kits or product bundles nearby to encourage larger purchases. Provide clear instructions on how to place orders or sign up as a customer or team member.

To create a successful booth on a budget, prioritize versatility and simplicity. I would also suggest easy to transport in and out. Opt for DIY display options using affordable materials like PVC pipes or fabric. Look for cost-effective ways to brand your booth, such as online printing services or reusable signage. Choose lightweight, portable display elements that can be set up quickly and easily. Following these tips, you can create a visually appealing booth that attracts attention, engages attendees, and drives sales at vendor shows.

Strategic Inventory Planning for Vendor Events

Once you've secured a spot at a vendor event and are ready to showcase your products or services, strategic inventory planning becomes crucial for maximizing your success. By aligning your inventory with the event's theme, considering seasonal trends, and leveraging your branding, you can optimize your stock levels to meet demand effectively. Here's how you can make informed decisions about how much inventory to bring while avoiding the pitfalls of overstocking.

Firstly, take the theme of the event into account. Whether it's a holiday market, a health and wellness expo, or a craft fair, tailoring your inventory to fit the theme can significantly enhance your appeal to attendees. Focus on products that align with the event's theme and resonate with the interests and preferences of the target audience. For example, if it's a holiday market, prioritize seasonal items or gift-worthy products that capture the festive spirit.

Secondly, consider the season of the year when planning your inventory. Seasonal trends and weather conditions can influence consumer behavior and product preferences. For instance, lightweight clothing, outdoor accessories, and skincare products may be in high demand during summer. In contrast, as the temperatures drop in the winter, cozy apparel, cold-weather gear, and holiday-themed gift items may take precedence. Adjust your inventory accordingly to capitalize on seasonal opportunities and meet the needs of attendees.

Additionally, leverage your branding to guide inventory decisions. Your brand identity, values, and target audience should inform the types of products you offer and the quantity of inventory you bring to the event. Consider your brand's unique selling proposition (USP) and the preferences of your target demographic. If your brand emphasizes sustainability, prioritize Eco-friendly products. If affordability is a key selling point, focus on offering budget-friendly options.

While it's essential to be prepared and adequately stocked for the event, avoiding overstocking and overwhelming customers is equally important. Start with a conservative inventory level based on thorough market research, past sales data for the event, and anticipated foot traffic. You can ask the vendor coordinator about previous information. Use sales performance during the event to rotate or add more items if you have them and adjust inventory levels to balance supply and demand.

Strategic inventory planning becomes even more critical for multi-day events. Continuously monitor sales trends and adjust inventory levels daily to ensure a steady supply of popular items without excess inventory carrying over to subsequent days. Consider offering special promotions or discounts towards the end of the event to clear out remaining inventory and maximize sales opportunities.

In summary, strategic inventory planning involves considering the event's theme, seasonal trends, and branding to determine the optimal mix and quantity of products to bring. By aligning your inventory with the interests and preferences of attendees and staying adaptable throughout the event, you can optimize your inventory management practices and maximize your sales potential at vendor events.

The Day Before & Day of

Preparing for a successful vendor event involves more than just setting up your booth; it's about getting yourself in the right mindset and taking care of your well-being. As you set up your booth, immerse yourself in a bubble of happy music to boost your mood and energy levels. Prioritize getting a good night's sleep, staying hydrated, and eating nourishing meals to ensure you're physically and mentally prepared for the day ahead.

If you're setting up on the same day as the event, arrive early to allow ample time for setup and to connect with fellow vendors. Hand out special sample packets to your neighboring vendors as a gesture of goodwill and camaraderie, whether candy for a sweet treat or stress relief items to help them through the day. Be proactive in preparing for any weather conditions by updating your booth with cooling options for hot days or bringing extra rain ponchos for potential rain showers. Try to befriend the vendors next to you, as they can provide support and camaraderie throughout the event.

Finally, ensure you have a well-stocked event emergency kit in your car, including essentials like scissors, tape, first aid supplies, and other items that may come in handy. By taking these steps to prepare yourself mentally and practically, you'll be ready to make the most of your participation in the event and ensure a successful experience for yourself and your fellow vendors.

Sasha's Do Not Leave Home Without These Essential Must-Have Items for a Good Day

Here's a list of essential items to bring to a vendor event booth, whether it's for a single-day or multiple-day event:

1. **Tablecloth or covering:** Provides a clean and professional appearance for your booth setup. My sneaky trick if you can not get a logo tablecloth due to time or funds is a twin flat sheet in black. It is often cheap from Walmart, Target, or a discount household store.
2. **Signage and banners:** Display your brand name, logo, and key messages to attract attention. Occasionally, with companies with a high turnover for products, you may want to be cautious with products being the main focus of the banners. I like to use banners for central brand values or fast facts that someone can read in a few seconds, including visuals or icons they would recognize from afar.

3. **Product displays:** Showcase your merchandise effectively with shelving units, racks, or stands.

4. **Inventory:** Sufficient stock of your products to meet demand throughout the event.

5. **Payment processing system:** Cash register & lock box with change of $20, credit card reader, or mobile payment device to accept various forms of payment.

6. **Business cards:** Provide potential customers with contact information and a way to follow up after the event.

7. **Promotional materials:** Fliers, brochures, or catalogs highlighting your products or services and including special offers or discounts.

8. **Samples or testers:** Allow customers to experience your products firsthand before purchasing. I like to ensure these have bright and clear stickers to prevent people from opening up your items for sale.

9. **Table and chairs:** Provide a comfortable space for engaging with customers and conducting transactions. Get a good chair with cup holders; it is needed.

10. **Packaging materials:** Bags, boxes, or gift wraps for customers to take their purchases home.

11. **Tools and supplies:** Tape, scissors, zip ties, and other essentials for booth setup, repairs, and maintenance.

12. **Storage containers:** Keep your booth organized and tidy with bins or crates for storing inventory, supplies, and personal belongings. I like to make sure these are clean. They can look rough after summer events in parking lots and grass fields.

13. **Refreshments:** Bottled water, snacks, and beverages to keep you energized and hydrated throughout the event.

14. **Backup power source:** Portable charger or extra batteries for electronic devices such as smartphones, tablets, or POS systems. (Half my friends just laughed because I am NOTORIOUS for having a dead phone)

15. **First aid kit:** Basic supplies for addressing minor injuries, blisters, break ice packs, or emergencies that may occur during the event.

By ensuring you have these essential items on hand, you'll be well-prepared to run a successful vendor event booth, whether it's for a single-day or multi-day event.

Following Up Afterward

Following up after holding an in-person vendor event is important to maintaining connections with attendees and converting interest into sales. Here are some touch points that a person can utilize for effective follow-up:

1. **Thank-You Email**: Send a personalized thank-you email to all attendees, expressing gratitude for their participation and support. Include a brief recap of the event highlights and any special offers or promotions discussed during the event.

2. **Social Media Engagement**: Connect with attendees on social media platforms like LinkedIn, X, or Facebook. Like, comment on, or share their posts about the event, and initiate conversations to keep the interaction going.

3. **Follow-Up Survey**: Send a follow-up survey to gather feedback on the event experience. Ask attendees about their favorite parts of the event, areas for improvement, and their level of interest in the products or services showcased.

4. **Personalized Follow-Up Calls**: Reach out to attendees individually via phone calls to thank them for attending and discuss their experience further. Use this opportunity to address any questions or concerns they may have and guide them toward making a purchase.

5. **Email Newsletter Subscription**: Encourage event attendees to subscribe to your email newsletter for updates, promotions, and exclusive content related to your products or services. Provide a clear call-to-action and incentive for subscribing, such as a special welcome offer.

6. **Product Demonstrations or Samples**: Offer to provide product demonstrations or samples to attendees who expressed interest in specific products or services during the event. This allows them to

experience the offerings firsthand and can increase their likelihood of making a purchase.

7. **Exclusive Offers or Discounts**: Offer exclusive discounts or special offers to event attendees as a token of appreciation for their participation. This can incentivize them to purchase and capitalize on the interest generated during the event.

8. **Referral Program**: Encourage event attendees to refer friends or family members to your business in exchange for rewards or incentives. Offer a referral program where the referrer and the new customer benefit from successful referrals.

9. **Post-Event Follow-Up Email Series**: Implement a post-event email series to nurture leads and guide them through sales. Provide valuable content, testimonials, and success stories related to your products or services to keep attendees engaged and interested.

10. **Virtual Follow-Up Event or Q&A Session**: Host a virtual follow-up event or Q&A session for event attendees to further engage with your brand and products. Use this opportunity to provide additional information, answer questions, and showcase new offerings or updates.

Utilizing these touch points for follow-up after holding an in-person vendor event can maintain engagement, nurture leads, and drive sales conversion.

Rocking Event Sales

Participating in festivals, fairs, and events presents a prime opportunity for vendors to showcase their products or services and drive sales. To maximize your success at these events, following best practices that engage attendees, maintaining a professional presence, and capitalizing on every sales opportunity are essential.

Avoid the temptation to sit behind your booth – standing allows you to appear approachable and ready to assist potential customers. Keep your energy levels high by staying active and engaged throughout the event, greeting attendees with a smile, and initiating conversations as they pass by. Starting conversations with people walking by your booth is essential to drawing them in and generating interest in your products or services. A simple greeting or compliment can serve as an icebreaker to initiate a conversation. Ask open-ended questions to learn more about attendees' interests and needs, allowing you to tailor your pitch accordingly.

While staying present at your booth is essential, taking care of your needs is also important. Coordinate with neighboring vendors or event staff to watch your booth briefly while you take a quick bathroom break. Plan your breaks strategically during slower periods to minimize disruptions to your sales flow. Take advantage of opportunities to reach attendees beyond the confines of your booth by requesting to include information or promotional items in event swag bags. This allows you to extend your reach and ensure that even those who may not have visited your booth directly are exposed to your brand and offerings. Consider including a special offer or incentive to encourage recipients to visit your booth during the event.

Presenting a polished and professional image will instill confidence in potential customers and build trust in your brand. Ensure your booth is tidy and well-organized, with clear signage and displays highlighting your products or services. Dress appropriately for the event, reflecting the style and tone of your brand while prioritizing comfort and practicality. Don't let the connection end once the event is over. Collect contact information from interested attendees and follow up with personalized messages or offers to continue the conversation and nurture potential leads. Express appreciation for their interest in your brand and products, and offer assistance or additional information to engage them further and drive sales.

Implementing these best practices can enhance vendors' presence at festivals, fairs, and events and maximize their sales success. From staying active and engaged at the booth to initiating conversations with attendees and leveraging opportunities for extended outreach, these strategies help vendors maximize their participation and drive meaningful business results.

9

Online & In-Person Parties

P arties, whether online or in person, are what you make of them. If you approach them with excitement and creativity, they can be engaging and memorable experiences for you and your guests. Gone are the days when parties were synonymous with dull presentations and awkward social interactions. As someone who once dreaded hosting or attending parties, I understand the stigma they carried for many years. It seemed like a tedious task of holding a group of strangers captive while flipping through a booklet of information, hardly an appealing way to spend a Saturday.

As a military wife, I've been to my fair share of skincare lessons and sit-down dinners with beer bread, where the atmosphere often felt forced and impersonal. However, amongst the monotony, there were moments of delight, like the party with chocolate martinis, that I couldn't help but enjoy. It became clear to me that parties have the potential to be so much more than just a sales pitch or a social obligation—they can be opportunities for genuine connection, laughter, and shared experiences. With the right approach and a touch of creativity, parties can become powerful tools for building relationships and growing your brand.

Finding Events or Hosts

Finding hosts excited about our brand and products is super important for our Facebook or online parties to be a hit. Here's how you can find hosts pumped to earn product credit by sharing our link and inviting their friends to check out what we offer.

First, ask people you know who've shown interest in what we sell. Maybe they've bought from us before, or they follow us online. They might be interested in hosting a party to get some freebies.

Next, create posts on your social media inviting your followers to become hosts. Tell them about the perks like getting free products, special discounts, and being the first to try new stuff. You can sweeten the deal by offering extra goodies for those who sign up to host. Think of it as a thank-you for helping us out.

If you have friends who've hosted parties before, ask them to spread the word to their friends who might be interested. We'll even give them a little bonus if they bring in new hosts.

And if you know any famous people online who talk about things like ours, see if they'd like to team up. They can tell their followers about hosting parties for us, reaching even more potential hosts.

Lastly, consider hosting special events just for people interested in becoming hosts. Use these events to show off our products, explain how hosting works, and answer any questions they might have.

By doing these things, hosts will be excited to earn product credit by inviting their friends to our Facebook or online parties.

Filling in Your Calendar

When you decide to host parties, whether online or in person, planning them wisely on your calendar is essential. Think of your calendar as your business storefront—the more events you have, the longer your door opens for people to learn about your offerings.

Consider the duration of your parties carefully. Some last just one hour, while others span a week or two. The length of your party depends on your goals and your audience's preferences. For example, if you're targeting military families who get paid on the first and fifteenth of the month, scheduling your parties around those paydays can increase attendance and sales.

For month-long parties, you can send out samples and give participants enough time to receive them and engage in posts that reference these samples. This extended time frame allows for a more relaxed pace, enabling participants to interact with your content conveniently.

It's important to remember that not every party will result in immediate sales. Booking parties early in the month gives you more time to follow up with hosts and participants who may need reminders or additional assistance. This proactive approach can help maximize your sales and engagement opportunities.

Additionally, consider your company's reward structure. Some companies offer rewards based on calendar months, while others focus on sales levels regardless of the month those sales occur. If your company operates on a calendar month basis, ensuring that your parties span the entire month is a great way to take full advantage of customer specials and incentives.

By carefully planning the duration and timing of your parties and aligning them with paydays and reward structures, you can optimize your chances of success and maximize your business opportunities.

Signage and Graphics.

At your parties, signage or graphics can go a long way in streamlining communication, creating brand recognition, and creating a welcoming atmosphere for your guests. Taking the time to position signs or graphics that reflect your company's values and identity will not only save you from the pressure of explaining these concepts verbally. Still, it will also ensure that guests are immersed in the essence of your brand from the moment they step in. Imagine a beautifully designed sign welcoming guests with a brief statement about your company's mission or values. This will set a tone of authenticity and professionalism, laying the foundation for meaningful interactions throughout the party. Using well-placed logos and strategically placed QR codes linked to a Google form near the entrance, you can seamlessly collect guest information without interrupting the flow of conversation.

Throughout the party, signage can inform guests about the host incentive program and provide information on joining. This will make it easy for guests to explore opportunities without feeling pressured or overwhelmed. As guests mingle and socialize, they can effortlessly navigate through the sales funnel, guided by strategically placed graphics that introduce products and showcase deals. This laid-back approach ensures that guests feel empowered to engage at their own pace while you focus on building genuine connections and facilitating a memorable experience for everyone. With signage and graphics communicating essential information, you can relax and enjoy the party, knowing that guests receive a cohesive and impactful message about your brand and offerings.

Connecting at an In-Person Party

Some of my most successful and fun moments in this industry were sitting on the ground gossiping with women while they soaked their feet trying out my products. In-home parties are often looked at like they need to be complicated presentations of every product you sell when it really should just feel like you are hanging out with your friends.

Here's a natural and low-pressure outline for a successful in-person party at a host's house:

1. **Welcome and Socializing (15 minutes)**: Start the party by warmly welcoming everyone as they arrive. Encourage guests to mingle, chat, and enjoy light refreshments. Use this time to build rapport and make everyone feel comfortable.
2. **Introduction and Icebreaker Activity (10 minutes)**: Introduce yourself and briefly share your connection to the company and its products. Break the ice with a fun activity or game that involves everyone interacting.
3. **Product Demonstration (20 minutes)**: Showcase the company's main

products or categories. Allow guests to touch, smell, and try out the products themselves. Share personal anecdotes or testimonials to highlight the products' benefits and features.

4. **Interactive Session (15 minutes)**: Engage guests in an interactive session where they can ask questions or share their thoughts and experiences. Encourage discussion and feedback in a relaxed and open environment.

5. **Special Offers and Discounts (10 minutes)**: Introduce any special offers, discounts, or promotions exclusively for party attendees. Highlight the value proposition and savings they can enjoy by purchasing products during the party.

6. **Hostess Rewards and Booking Opportunities (10 minutes)**: Thank the host for hosting the party and explain the rewards they can earn based on party sales. Invite guests to consider hosting their parties and explain the benefits and rewards of becoming a hostess.

7. **Closing Remarks and Thank You (5 minutes)**: Thank everyone for attending the party and their interest in the products. Provide contact information for follow-up questions or orders. Encourage guests to take advantage of any remaining time to revisit products or chat with you one-on-one.

By following this outline, you can create a relaxed and enjoyable atmosphere where guests can explore the products at their own pace without feeling pressured to make a purchase. The focus is on building connections, providing valuable information, and offering an authentic and engaging experience for everyone involved.

Planning and keeping things simple is essential for someone new to hosting in-home parties. Start by setting a date, inviting guests, and outlining a primary agenda for the event. When the day arrives, focus on creating a welcoming atmosphere with lighting, music, and comfortable seating arrangements. Throughout the party, engage with your guests, answer their questions, and share your excitement about the products. Provide samples and demonstrations to allow guests to experience the products firsthand and encourage participation through interactive activities or games. After the party, follow up with guests to thank them for attending and address any additional inquiries they may have.

Regarding safety, ensure that your home is clean and free of hazards, especially if serving food or drinks. Be mindful of guests' dietary restrictions or allergies and provide suitable options. During the COVID-19 pandemic, adhere to local health guidelines and implement measures such as mask-wearing and social distancing as necessary. Offer hand sanitizer and encourage good hygiene practices among guests. If handling products or demonstrations, follow safety precautions and instructions provided by the company. By adhering to these best practices and safety tips, you can host a successful in-home party while prioritizing the well-being and comfort of your guests.

Creating Scripts for Online Parties

Once you have an online party host and the date is set, it is time to craft a party script that will knock their socks off. There are many ways to do this so that I will share a few versions with you. Feel free to pick the best one for you and your audience to make the best connection.

The most basic version of a party script for a party involves planning each event day's content and engagement activities. Here's a step-by-step process to guide you through it:

1. **Set Objectives**: Begin by defining the objectives of your party. What do you hope to achieve? Whether it's increasing product sales, generating leads, or recruiting new team members, having clear objectives will shape your party script.
2. **Outline Daily Themes**: Decide on a theme for each party day. This could include product spotlights, customer testimonials, behind-the-scenes content, interactive games, live demonstrations, or Q&A sessions. Themes help keep the party engaging and cohesive.
3. **Create Content for Each Day**: Create content for each party day

based on your themes. This could include text posts, images, videos, polls, quizzes, and interactive posts. Be creative and provide valuable information about your products or business opportunities.

4. **Incorporate Engagement Activities**: Plan engagement activities to keep participants involved throughout the week. Encourage likes, comments, shares, and participation in games or challenges. This could include asking questions, inviting feedback, or running contests with prizes.

5. **Include Calls to Action**: Throughout your party script, incorporate clear calls to action (CTAs), prompting participants to take the next step, whether purchasing, joining your team, or booking their party. Provide links and instructions to make it easy for them to respond.

6. **Schedule Posts**: Use Facebook's scheduling feature to plan and schedule your posts in advance. This ensures consistency and lets you focus on engaging with participants in real time during the party.

7. **Prepare Graphics and Visuals**: Create eye-catching graphics and visuals to accompany your posts. Use images, GIFs, infographics, and videos to capture attention and enhance your message.

8. **Draft Introduction and Closing Posts**: Start and end your party with a warm welcome and a heartfelt thank you. Your introduction post sets the tone for the party, while your closing post expresses gratitude and provides the next steps for participants.

9. **Review and Revise**: Before the party begins, review your script to ensure it flows smoothly and aligns with your objectives. Based on feedback or changing circumstances, make any necessary revisions or adjustments.

10. **Monitor and Engage**: During the party, actively monitor participant engagement, respond to comments and questions, and adapt your script to keep the momentum going.

By following these steps, you can create a well-structured and engaging party script for your Facebook party, maximizing your chances of success and creating a positive experience for participants.

Now, let's take this to the next level. Have you ever taken an online test to see what cheese flavor your personality is? That sounds silly, but personality tests are a fantastic way to bond with strangers very quickly, and this is where my friend, Mandi Howard, was inspired to develop a party script style that we call Game Nights. It is a style of party that is heavily engaging and can take the form of a million themes over time. I have used it successfully and adjusted it to my personality to incorporate the sales funnel better.

Here is the backbone format of a Game Night style online script, and you will recognize that the information being shared, in a fun way, is the information needed to help someone move through the sales funnel process:

PRE-PARTY INFORMATION POSTS LEADING UP TO THE PARTY:

- **Post 1 What is (your company or brand)?** This post includes a concise explanation of your company and its values. The more elevator pitch type of information, the better.
- **Post 2 Who has tried (your company or brand)?** This is an engagement post to get your guests to say Yes or No and then request the samples you send to guests.
- **Post 3 How Does This Event Work?** This post establishes clear expectations for your guests, including the party shopping link and shipping deadlines, restrictions on sample packet availability to instill a sense of urgency, and the schedule for posts on the day of the party.
- **Post 4 All About You.** This post is a game post with which you can engage guests to bond over the theme or a fun fact.
- **Post 5 Giveaway.** Based on your company and what your Policies and Procedures allow on social media, this post explains any giveaways you will have during the event for comments, likes, or orders placed.
- **Post 6 Specials.** You do not have to hold a giveaway; this can also be a great place to discuss company-specific discounts or deals for specific free shipping or sales levels. I like to include discounts for the military or specifics if a product is launched when the party link is open.

PARTY POSTS ON THE PARTY DAY

- **Post 1-3 one-hour, 30-minute, and five-minute warning** graphic posts: These posts help people prepare for the Game Nights. I also challenge people to post selfies with their drinks or ask how their day was.

- **Post 4 "Ready, Set, Go" Post:** This helps to remind them to refresh their page for new posts every 5 minutes.

- **Post 5-10 6 Product or Theme Posts**: I use these to tell a story, create a scene, or craft a product bundle. In this party section, they comment on the letter from multiple-choice captions they most commonly relate to. On the graphics, I line up the answers to the answer key that asks them if they got mostly A's, B's, C's, or D's to determine their answer.

- **Post 11: The answer key** includes four personality types that match the four central values of my company's products. The letter A tends to be the most useful, resourceful, or hard-working product choice. The letter B has a comforting and nurturing theme. Letter C represents bold trending items that are more innovative. Lastly, the letter D leans toward a free spirit that is more on the go, classic, or clean products. I repeat personality types in these four squares when incorporating themes like holiday food or movie characters.

- **Post 12 Join My VIP:** Once you have bonded with your guests over relatable topics, products, and themes, it is a great time to help them stay connected with you so that they can continue to grow a relationship outside of the first party they attend with you. You can have them join your VIP group, newsletter, text service, or whatever you have decided is the best way to hang out with you.

- **Post 13 Specials:** In the next post, remind them about the specials you mentioned over the first few days of connecting to bring that information back to the forefront while they consider purchasing from you.

- **Post 14 Host or Join:** By far the scariest of questions for many, I find the best time to ask if they want to host a party or join is during the part of the party that they are considering a purchase, just like in the sale funnels. My company allows consultants to host events, so I like to explain all the advantages of hosting, then add in the commissions and jump-start the total so they get the picture that hosts can get even more if they join and launch their business with the party. It is a post that begins our conversation about layering deals and discounts to launch a business strong in Chapter 3 early in the relationship!

- **Post 15 Thank them!** Gratitude is always the best way to leave someone you connect with, even if they do not purchase. Thank them for spending time with you, trying the samples, and hanging out for the party.

After the party posts are over for the night, I like to let the algorithm do its work. I will start posting a few days later so that the posts have time to appear on the feeds of anyone who missed them. It is also a chance for people to go back in and comment if they miss or participate in any challenges.

Once the party night is over, you may have more time in the month to foster connection. This is an excellent time for hilarious but professional memes that go with your theme, more ingredient facts, or engagement questions asking for feedback and testimonials about the samples you sent.

Following Up Afterward

Following up after holding an online or in-person party is essential for maintaining engagement and converting interest into sales. Here are some touch points that a person can utilize for effective follow-up:

1. **Thank-You Email**: Send a personalized thank-you email to all attendees, expressing gratitude for their participation and support. Include a brief recap of the event highlights and any special offers or promotions discussed during the event.
2. **Social Media Engagement**: Engage with attendees on social media platforms like Facebook, Instagram, or X. Like, comment on, or share their posts about the event, and initiate conversations to keep the

interaction going.

3. **Follow-Up Survey**: Send a follow-up survey to gather feedback on the event experience. Ask attendees about their favorite parts of the event, areas for improvement, and their level of interest in the products or services showcased.

4. **Exclusive Offers or Discounts**: Offer exclusive discounts or special offers to event attendees as a token of appreciation for their participation. This can incentivize them to purchase and capitalize on the interest generated during the event.

5. **Product Demonstrations or Samples**: Offer to provide product demonstrations or samples to attendees who expressed interest in specific products or services during the event. This allows them to experience the offerings firsthand and can increase their likelihood of making a purchase.

6. **Personalized Follow-Up Calls or Messages**: Contact attendees individually via phone calls or direct messages to thank them for attending and discuss their experience further. Use this opportunity to address any questions or concerns they may have and guide them toward making a purchase.

7. **Email Newsletter Subscription**: Encourage event attendees to subscribe to your email newsletter for updates, promotions, and exclusive content related to your products or services. Provide a clear call-to-action and incentive for subscribing, such as a special welcome offer.

8. **Virtual Follow-Up Event or Q&A Session**: Host a virtual follow-up event or Q&A session for event attendees to further engage with your brand and products. Use this opportunity to provide additional information, answer questions, and showcase new offerings or updates.

9. **Referral Program**: Encourage party attendees to refer friends or family members to your business in exchange for rewards or incentives. Offer a referral program in which both the referrer and the new customer benefit from successful referrals.

10. **Post-Party Follow-Up Email Series**: Implement a post-party email series to nurture leads and guide them through sales. Provide valuable

content, testimonials, and success stories related to your products or services to keep attendees engaged and interested.

By utilizing these touch points for follow-up after holding an online or in-person party, you can effectively maintain engagement, nurture leads, and drive sales conversion.

10

Navigating Leadership As A Beginner

We've been through a lot together and are now at a big moment. You've gotten yourself out there, built your brand, and figured out social media in a way that even a tech expert would be impressed by. You've done something unique: someone brave has joined your team.

Leadership is multifaceted, and styles range from micromanagement to laissez-faire. In layperson's terms, some leaders require more control and feedback than others. Leaders can be inspiring and approachable, while others can be demanding and professionally standoffish. Instead of worrying about the intricacies of leadership, let's take a breath and appreciate this moment: You're officially a leader. It's exciting and quite scary, but it can also be rewarding.

Regarding my leadership style, I apply an adaptive style that spans the spectrum at appropriate times. I believe in putting people first and allowing them to excel at their strengths. It doesn't matter if it's my customers, hosts, teammates, or new folks joining the crew; I have come to the understanding that it's the people who make this business profitable and enjoyable.

Considering the many aspects of leadership, relationship building seems to be the ongoing and common thread to the success of your business and your team. Relationships are complicated and can be influenced by all sorts of things we can see and the stuff we can't. Understanding that you cannot approach leadership as a simple step-by-step process will prepare you for dealing with and managing all the nuances of relationship and team building, delegation of training, and knowing when it's time to let your leaders lead.

First Impressions

Starting a new professional relationship can be similar to going on a first date—it's exciting but also nerve-wracking. You and your date are essentially strangers, knowing little about each other, so making an excellent first impression is the primary goal. Like all first dates, asking them questions is necessary to learn about common ground, personal values, and things they might enjoy. In a leadership role, there's a similar process of getting acquainted with your teammates or addressing new teammate concerns: Communication. Communication is paramount to any relationship, and this is especially true for all leaders. Having a set time of availability, clear avenues to express concerns or ask questions, and a productive environment for two-way feedback will be essential to your success. Always remember that it is vital for a leader to establish clear and reasonable expectations through effective communication and show that you are willing to invest time in your team's success and your teammate's success.

Connecting

Building rapport with your new teammate can only be accomplished through communication and bonding. In the early stages of 'dating,' you're putting your best foot forward, exploring new opportunities together, and striving to find compatible traits. As more time is spent "bonding," your teammates will develop a sense of cohesion and belonging. Through continued communication, you will learn more about your teammate's strengths and weaknesses. You will learn how to motivate them and connect in a way that speaks to their personality.

As you know how to utilize their strengths best, your role will shift from hand-holding to providing support from the sidelines. This will help them to gain independence, continue to grow as a brand, and prepare to be a future leader. Connecting with your teammates as a leader should be a transitional flow throughout the leadership spectrum. Like the sales funnel, it is a cyclic, situationally dependent process, and only time and experience will help you develop your style. So please take it in and embrace your new responsibility. You will be free to repeat this cycle for each new teammate who joins and hone your skills.

Many aspects of leadership tie into connecting, but nothing is more important than public acknowledgment and praise. Publicly praising individuals for their successes and achievements boosts esteem and creates a nurturing environment. Public praise shows each person that you trust how they represent your brand and the team brand. Take every opportunity to praise your teammates' successes and hard work. Doing so will let them know you are watching and rooting for them. Public support and praise are fundamental to fostering trust in your team and trust amongst your teammates will ultimately lead to your overall success and profitability.

Fostering Trust

Let's dive into the most essential part of the leader-subordinate relationship: trust. Trust is more than one's faith in your abilities; your team believes you possess integrity and are credible, knowledgeable, selfless, and experienced. As your relationship with your new teammate progresses, akin to moving from dating to engagement, your commitment to the team will grow. At the same time, the intricacies of everyone's roles continue to develop. As you learn about each individual and their strengths, you may give more credence to traits and values that were previously overlooked and unnecessary at that time. Developments such as these are how you can continue to foster trust; you may offer up more opportunities for teammates to train others, invite them to participate in brainstorming sessions or provide a chance to create marketing materials for the team. You may realize, at this point, that you are delegating some of your responsibilities. Fostering trust allows this to occur, and trust affords you and your teammates the leverage to build and manage a larger team. With increased leadership responsibility and the necessity to delegate, you and your teammates will assess each other's performance and leadership styles more critically. It's not uncommon for tensions to rise as more chefs enter the kitchen, so maintaining open lines of communication and dispelling gossip will be necessary for the team's success in the broader context of the business. You will never be able to stop gossip, but you can prevent it from reaching public spaces and negatively impacting the team. Open lines of communication will result in unsolicited feedback, requests for additional training, workload adjustments, or less leadership interaction, but addressing these needs requires trust and mutual understanding. Remember not to take feedback as a personal attack on you as a leader. No one is perfect, and we don't know what we don't know until we learn about it. When your teammates see tangible results from your guidance and feel heard in their requests, they are more inclined to view you as a leader worth following, thereby gaining their trust.

Commitment

As the relationship with your new teammate grows, you will eventually reach the stage of 'marriage' in a traditional business context, where longevity and stability become paramount to success. This marks a significant milestone in your long-term team-building and business growth plan. While some individuals grasp this commitment from the outset and embrace it fully, others may take longer (trust is still being developed). During the commitment stage, there are many things to consider. As you have, your teammate will dedicate more of their efforts to the business, perhaps even relinquishing side ventures or making substantial financial decisions. Throughout this period, it's important to remind your teammate to maintain vigilance and avoid complacency. Remind your newly committed team member to make financial decisions based on data rather than emotions. Doing so will help them avoid being overwhelmed by debt. Debt is inadvertently caused by purchasing too much inventory or attending incentive trips beyond their means. This phase will represent a profound partnership in the business realm, demanding a corresponding level of dedication and responsibility fostered by the absolute trust built amongst your team. This period also marks a transition where leaders guide their teams and teammates to demonstrate self-leadership, ensuring alignment with organizational objectives, personal growth, and the brand.

Disconnecting

Inevitably, there comes a stage in business relationships—akin to the break-up or divorce phase in relationships—where parties may choose to part ways. Drawing from personal experiences of witnessing rapid friendship implosions, I can relate to the complexities of such transitions. People will leave your team for one reason or another, and it's essential not to take the break-up personally. There is a saying in the workforce, "You don't quit your job; you quit your boss." Teammate departures aren't very dissimilar to someone quitting their job. Some depart after leveraging their acquired knowledge to embark on entrepreneurial endeavors, while others exit disgruntled due to unmet expectations and needs. Regardless, it's imperative to acknowledge that life moves on. Such departures may also be triggered by evolving leadership styles within the team, where some seek to emulate mentors or rebel against existing norms to solidify their role as leaders and form their crew. This dynamic is reminiscent of generational patterns in family relationships, where rebellious tendencies often echo across leadership chains. Similar to the stories of the rebellious mother-daughter relationships down the family tree. While it may feel personal when faced with rebellion, it's essential to understand that it's usually a natural part of individual growth and development. Lingering in toxic relationships or workplaces only exacerbates the situation, akin to parents fighting in front of their children. Deciding when and how to navigate such separations is a challenging yet necessary aspect of leadership, guided by organizational needs and on par with your brand. While difficult decisions may lead to temporary hurt, focusing on the broader objectives ensures eventual stability and growth. Ultimately, resilience and a long-term perspective are vital to weathering such transitions, reassuring oneself that everything will be alright.

The cradle-to-grave dating analogy holds remarkably well when dissecting the intricacies of leadership in the direct sales industry. It's fascinating! While it's true that this analogy doesn't encompass all aspects of leadership—I could quickly write an entire book on various leadership styles, types of motivation, and organizational systems. It is a project I plan to undertake, but let's focus on the present. Please take a moment to reflect on how you lead your life; often, people overlook their potential and fail to recognize the importance of the relationships with those they work with. Acknowledge that everyone has flaws, and it's essential to support them to the best of your ability proactively. If your efforts resonate with them, that's wonderful. If not, rest assured you've done your utmost and adapted.

Remember, you can become anything, including an exceptional leader. It starts with opening your heart and seeking out resources. You can enhance your listening skills, increase your efforts, and deliberate more thoughtfully. You're capable of this.

11

Embracing Growth and Transformation

Here are all the lessons I learned along the way:

1. If you can dream it, you can do it.

I did one of those silly Pinterest crafts a long time ago where you pick a quote, put stickers on a canvas, and paint over the stickers. Then, you peel off the stickers, revealing a quote I would stare at for hours when I had no clue what to do next. I painted it rainbow colors like pixie dust and magic; it would remind me that, like the Walt Disney legacy, there will be ideas and dreams that many won't believe in. No one needs to believe in what you are doing except for you. Pick a quote and put it on your wall, fridge, or mirror. Right now.

2. If you do not know how to do something, there is always a way to learn. Accessibility to resources is more prevalent now than ever. On my frugal days, I will bring a mug of coffee and stand in the business section of the local library or peruse the internet. Figure out your favorite spot and MOVE in. You can take a book off the shelf at a chain or local bookstore, walk into the cafe, get free water, and sit there from open to closed, broadening your knowledge. Martin Luther King Jr told us, "If you can't fly, run. If you can't run, then walk. If you can't walk, then crawl, but keep moving." Search the internet for free copies if you cannot get to the library. If you can't stack up books, get an Amazon Kindle account. You get an audiobook version if you cannot sit and read. If you cannot read well, watch a video on YouTube. If you cannot watch a video, take a local class. Do your best with what you have so you can learn more.

3. Ask for help until you get it. If you do not reach out, you will not receive help. People want to help each other; people have experience and can help. YOU HAVE TO ASK. If the first person doesn't help you, keep going. You keep asking. You find the right one to stop and help. If you give up because one person will not help you succeed, you give up on your future self. In your heart, I am confident; you know that no one wants you to fail. No one wants you to give up. Someone will always help. Customers, leaders, fellow business owners, fellow vendors, teammates, people walking down the street, ASK.

4. Know yourself and delegate your weaknesses. This one is tough because many of us have negative self-talk. There will be some situations and weaknesses you cannot teach yourself out of. Accept them and delegate if possible. If you suck at money, get a great accountant you can trust that is vetted. If you cannot work social media, hire a trustworthy and robust teen who will run it confidently with your brand in mind. If you suck at team building, find a person that doesn't and teach them sales. If you suck at sales but are great at building your team, find a person that doesn't and teach them how to team create. If you need more ideas, find people who have been in business longer and ask them questions. If you suck at something, you have two choices, continue to suck and seek help or learn how to get better, if possible.

5. Do not be scared to add new people to your circle. New people can be scary when you are overwhelmed and anxious to talk to people. The best way to beat fear is to do something difficult repeatedly until it is a habit. Go to meetups and be weird. Be your usual self and see who runs and who gets closer. Don't misunderstand, be professional. But do not show up and act like you are the only person fearing judgment. If we didn't all sweat from nerves, no one would have made deodorant. Set up an account on Meetup or find a local group on your social media. Your first meeting can even be Yoga. Meet people. The good ones don't bite as hard.

6. If you hate what you are doing, change how you do it and set a new goal. You do not have to be the person you were 5 minutes ago. Reinvent yourself until the outside matches your inside. Many leaders had joined multiple direct sales companies before they had the right fit. Many people in business have started various companies before perfecting their processes. No one expects a person to hit a home run the first time they step up to home plate in Baseball, so why would you expect that of yourself? Gain enough experience to be ready when the right product, service, or situation comes along.

7. Build relationships out of friendship, not only for sales. Not everyone will buy from you; not everyone should. Make friends with people first, and if they seem like a good fit, offer them products like you would with everyone else. Do not use friendships as a trap to sell to them and cut people off if they say no. People that are like that suck. Do not be that person.

8. You determine how high you fly based on how strong you believe your wings are. If you wake up daily saying you can't do something, you have a 100% chance of not doing something. Self-talk is the thing that will crush your dreams. Negativity from inside of you will come out. You will tell yourself to quit everything a thousand times; don't. Be a rebel. Look you in the face and say NOPE. Those statements are embedded in your mind and can limit your life. Even if you quit, it doesn't mean they will go away.

9. You can learn to be a good leader if your heart is right. For every person in the world, there is a different theory about what it takes to be a great leader. Many agree it boils down to heart and the courage to act. I am happy to fail every day at things if I know that I will wake up and try again. I am also pleased to see that I suck at things when I try new stuff because the courage to act and get in the ring is much more important than standing back and waiting to be perfect. You have to work on your instincts so they get stronger. You practice, you get back up, you go to parties that suck, empty events, and you try again. You keep going as long as you believe you are helping someone else have a better day than the last.

10. Do the things you think you cannot do purely for the confidence you get from completing the task, not the response. Experimenting with life can be fun. I attended Cape Cod Sea Camps in Brewster, MA, from 6th to 8th grade. We would sit in this cool theater daily for morning announcements and nighttime shows. The banner on the theater's top said I Can & I Will. We would earn awards, trophies, and achievements all summer, which always came back to that saying. It is incredible when you prove yourself and others wrong about your potential. Somewhere in your heart, you know what you can create. You know your potential to make this path your own; you have the strength to push back.

When I started this book, my biggest fear was failing to express and explain that I could do what I was doing. There is no particular club, no elite credit card, and no chosen few. It was hard work and not giving up that got me this far. Building up my company of passionate people took a lot of love. I cannot, for one second, shortchange myself on how essential having heart was in making things happen.

For example, I told myself I couldn't write a book, but I wrote one.

Now it is your turn. Whenever someone tells you that you can't do, won't do, shouldn't do, wouldn't do, or didn't do because it hasn't been done or they can't, you must shout it out very clearly:

I can do this! I will do this! I did this!

Epilogue

The crazy thing that happens after I talk about all this to people is they get this look on their faces like a bus flew by through the air. I want to be the first to tell you that this book is not meant to overwhelm you but to be a resource to come back to repeatedly. Start somewhere, go one step at a time, and take small bites. Do not attack this like you will be at the top of your game in a week. But also, don't go so slow that you lose momentum. Step by step, you will build an empire that is not ignorable. I expect you to find me with ink marks, scribbles, a highlighter, and dog ears. I do not want this book to be cherished but broken in and broken down. I want this to be information you read repeatedly, not because you can't remember it all but because you start to understand and crave the results around each turn. I only say that because I would do that to books when I started my first business. The info was so deep that I drank it all from the bathtub and spit it back onto my team pages and the laps of great friends.

So, if that is where you are at, be proud. You are about to dive into months or years of growth. I am over ten years in and still returning to the basics here. I'm always here if you need me. You can message me or chat on social media. You are strong. You can do this. I'll be watching with popcorn!

Afterword

Acknowledgments

To My Amazing Parents, Joe, Rob, Steve, and Susan! Life has not always been easy, but you have always tried your hardest to give me and our family every opportunity you could. Thank you a million times.

To my husband Dave and my babies, thank you for your patience and understanding while I hid in the basement and bathroom, building a business and this book on borrowed time. I hope you always know it was for our future, and I can't wait to find new ways to make life unforgettable as we all grow up.

To my family, thank you for always offering a kind word and reminding me that I can pull up my bootstraps and keep going. You are some of the strongest people in my life. Without learning from all of you, I wouldn't have the strength inside of me.

To my friends who helped me believe in myself and supported my many crazy ideas, you know who you are. Thanks for standing by me, occasionally laughing at the bad ideas, and always threatening me with a martini and a good time. We have been through so much; I am glad we have each other.

To Jess Mastorakos, thank you for answering all my messages about self-publishing. You have fantastic knowledge.

Special shouts to the Beta Readers and Volunteer editors Dave Sweder, Rob

Pastorio, Ronna Lebo, Shaylene Fisher, Jen Storm, Desiree Nudo, and Korrie Noelle. Thank you for the feedback and helping translate all this passion into words.

To my teammates who believed in a dream, thank you for trusting me as I have learned and grown.

To my sponsor, Lauren Rush, I can never repay you for the blessings you have brought. You are forever in my heart and my life, so you are stuck with me.

About the Author

You can connect with me on:

- 🌐 https://sashasweder.com
- 📘 https://www.facebook.com/SashaSweder1
- 📎 https://www.pinterest.com/SashaSweder1

www.ingramcontent.com/pod-product-compliance
Lightning Source LLC
Chambersburg PA
CBHW060325130626
46553CB00003B/917